D1240236

Samuel de Champlain: Founder of New France

A Brief History with Documents

Related Titles in
THE BEDFORD SERIES IN HISTORY AND CULTURE
Advisory Editors: Lynn Hunt, *University of California, Los Angeles*
David W. Blight, *Yale University*
Bonnie G. Smith, *Rutgers University*
Natalie Zemon Davis, *Princeton University*
Ernest R. May, *Harvard University*

Christopher Columbus and the Enterprise of the Indies: A Brief History with Documents
Geoffrey Symcox, *University of California, Los Angeles*, and Blair Sullivan, *University of California, Los Angeles*

Victors and Vanquished: Spanish and Nahua Views of the Conquest of Mexico
Edited with an Introduction by Stuart B. Schwartz, *Yale University*

Envisioning America: English Plans for the Colonization of North America, 1580–1640
Edited with an Introduction by Peter C. Mancall, *University of Southern California*

THE DISCOVERY OF GUIANA by Sir Walter Ralegh with Related Documents
Edited with an Introduction by Benjamin Schmidt, *University of Washington*

The World Turned Upside Down: Indian Voices from Early America
Edited with an Introduction by Colin G. Calloway, *Dartmouth College*

THE JESUIT RELATIONS: Natives and Missionaries in Seventeenth-Century North America
Edited with an Introduction by Allan Greer, *University of Toronto*

Manifest Destiny and American Territorial Expansion: A Brief History with Documents
Amy S. Greenberg, *Pennsylvania State University*

The Lewis and Clark Expedition: Selections from the Journals, Arranged by Topic
Edited with an Introduction by Gunther Barth, *University of California, Berkeley*

THE BEDFORD SERIES IN HISTORY AND CULTURE

Samuel de Champlain: Founder of New France

A Brief History with Documents

Gayle K. Brunelle

California State University, Fullerton

BEDFORD/ST. MARTIN'S   Boston ◆ New York

For Bedford/St. Martin's

Publisher for History: Mary V. Dougherty
Director of Development for History: Jane Knetzger
Senior Editor: Heidi L. Hood
Developmental Editor: Ann Kirby-Payne
Associate Editor: Jennifer Jovin
Editorial Assistant: Laura Kintz
Production Supervisor: Lisa Chow
Senior Marketing Manager: Amy Whitaker
Project Management: Books By Design, Inc.
Cartography: Mapping Specialists, Ltd.
Text Design: Claire Seng-Niemoeller
Cover Design: Marine Miller
Cover Art: "Carte geographique de la Nouvelle Franse faictte par le Sieur de Champlain Saint Tongois Cappitaine Ordinaire pour le Roy en la Marine," in Samuel de Champlain, *Les Voyages du Sieur de Champlain Xaintongeois, Capitaine ordinaire pour le Roy, en la marine. Divisez en deux livres. Ou, Journal tres-fidele des observations faites és descouvertures de la Nouvelle France* (Paris: Jean Berjon), 1613. Engraving based on an original map drawn by Champlain.
Composition: Achorn International, Inc.
Printing and Binding: RR Donnelley and Sons

President: Joan E. Feinberg
Editorial Director: Denise B. Wydra
Director of Marketing: Karen R. Soeltz
Director of Production: Susan W. Brown
Associate Director, Editorial Production: Elise S. Kaiser
Manager, Publishing Services: Andrea Cava

Library of Congress Control Number: 2011943868

Manufactured in the United States of America.

7   6   5   4   3   2
f   e   d   c   b   a

For information, write: Bedford / St. Martin's, 75 Arlington Street, Boston, MA 02116 (617-399-4000)

ISBN: 978-0-312-59263-9

Acknowledgments

Acknowledgments and copyrights are continued at the back of the book on page 133, which constitutes an extension of the copyright page.

Foreword

The Bedford Series in History and Culture is designed so that readers can study the past as historians do.

The historian's first task is finding the evidence. Documents, letters, memoirs, interviews, pictures, movies, novels, or poems can provide facts and clues. Then the historian questions and compares the sources. There is more to do than in a courtroom, for hearsay evidence is welcome, and the historian is usually looking for answers beyond act and motive. Different views of an event may be as important as a single verdict. How a story is told may yield as much information as what it says.

Along the way the historian seeks help from other historians and perhaps from specialists in other disciplines. Finally, it is time to write, to decide on an interpretation and how to arrange the evidence for readers.

Each book in this series contains an important historical document or group of documents, each document a witness from the past and open to interpretation in different ways. The documents are combined with some element of historical narrative—an introduction or a biographical essay, for example—that provides students with an analysis of the primary source material and important background information about the world in which it was produced.

Each book in the series focuses on a specific topic within a specific historical period. Each provides a basis for lively thought and discussion about several aspects of the topic and the historian's role. Each is short enough (and inexpensive enough) to be a reasonable one-week assignment in a college course. Whether as classroom or personal reading, each book in the series provides firsthand experience of the challenge—and fun—of discovering, recreating, and interpreting the past.

Lynn Hunt
David W. Blight
Bonnie G. Smith
Natalie Zemon Davis
Ernest R. May

Preface

Samuel de Champlain made twelve voyages to North America between 1603 and 1633. He authored four works that recounted his explorations and his struggle to found a French colony there and recorded his observations of the flora, fauna, and Native American peoples he encountered. Each volume was published in his own day and was lavishly illustrated with engravings and maps that provided the most accurate and informative depictions of North American geography then available. The works of Champlain also offer the best account we have of the conflict within seventeenth-century French society over whether and how France should colonize North America. His *Works* became increasingly popular after his death and ultimately shaped the founding narratives of the colonization of northeastern North America and the creation of New France.

Given the crucial historical role Champlain played in the histories of France and North America as well as the clarity of his writing style and the historical significance of his maps, it is surprising that so few of his works have been published in a format easily accessible to English-speaking students. As a result, relatively few students have had the opportunity to read firsthand Champlain's tales of exploration and encounters with North America and its peoples or to examine the groundbreaking maps he produced. This book provides both selections from Champlain's works and, in an introduction, an overview of Champlain's life and the historical context for his works. It is my hope that the book will introduce students of European, North American, or world history as well as those studying historical geography to Champlain and the role France played in the early history of North America and the construction of the Atlantic world. Students who read this book will gain insight into how Champlain's explorations and—perhaps more important—his maps and documentation of his exploits shaped perceptions about North America and its peoples, from his own day to the present. I hope this book will tempt students to venture further into the works and life of this flawed but interesting and intrepid man and the New France he helped to create.

It is impossible in a work of this length to cover every facet of Samuel de Champlain's eventful career or to include all the fascinating and rich material devoted to New France in the works he published. Here the goal is to highlight four central aspects of Champlain's accomplishments, each of which, with some overlap, loosely corresponds to a period in his life: his geographical explorations, his observations of and relationships with the Natives, his achievements in cartography, and finally, his career as a colonial administrator, lobbyist, and diplomat. Part One offers a thorough introduction that places Champlain in the contexts of his time, with helpful background on the history of French exploration and colonization in the New World, the unique relationships the French developed with specific Native tribes, and the political and economic realities that influenced Champlain's endeavors to establish New France. Part Two includes sixteen selections from Champlain's written works, including four period maps and three accompanying illustrations. Each document is introduced with a helpful headnote that puts the excerpt in context and illuminates some of the events described in it. Footnotes clarify references within the readings that may be unfamiliar to students.

Additional pedagogical aids support student understanding. A useful chronology highlights key events in Champlain's life, and questions for consideration invite students to compare and think critically about the documents. Finally, the selected bibliography provides additional sources for students who wish to research further.

A NOTE ABOUT THE TEXT

The documents in this book have been selected from the six-volume *Works of Samuel de Champlain* that H. P. Biggar edited in the first decades of the twentieth century, which remains the standard translation for most of Champlain's works to this day. Although the Biggar edition of Champlain's works is venerable and close to a century old, its English translations are still clear and crisp in their language and understandable to a college undergraduate. Champlain is particularly accessible to undergraduates compared to many writers of his day precisely because his training was as a soldier, and in personal expression he tended to be frank, forthright, even somewhat prosaic. His writing, as a result, lacks the rhetorical flourishes and classical allusions beloved of many of his contemporaries that can often make literature from the early modern era difficult for modern students to comprehend or appreciate. Champlain's wit is subtle, and, although he clearly liked a good story, he was not prone to dramatic embellishments of the events he recounts.

Champlain, in keeping with the nomenclature of his day, described the Native peoples he encountered as *sauvages*, which is usually translated in the documents according to its literal meaning of "savages." In some cases, he also refers to them as *Indians*. These references, of course, derive from his European ethnocentric biases, conscious and unconscious. Champlain observed the Natives as an outsider. He was unable to understand their languages, lacked a deep comprehension of their culture, and judged them according to the standards of European culture. But when he termed the Natives *savages*, he did not by any means intend to imply that they were not human, inferior in a biological or racial sense, or incapable of civilization. In the introduction and headnotes for this volume, I have endeavored to name specific tribes when possible to do so without confusing readers, since there were numerous tribes and subtribes with their own names they used to refer to themselves, which often vary in spelling. Otherwise, I use the relatively neutral term *Natives*, although there is also disagreement among contemporary Native peoples and among the scholars who study them as to the most appropriate general term to use when referring to them.

ACKNOWLEDGMENTS

I am extremely grateful to California State University, Fullerton, which provided me with crucial funding and sabbatical leave that permitted me to research and write this book. I would like to thank Mary Dougherty, the acquisitions editor at Bedford/St. Martin's, whose interest in this project got it underway, as well as Ann Kirby-Payne and Heidi Hood, whose patience helped guide me through the manuscript development process, and Andrea Cava, who shepherded it through production. I also thank Nancy Benjamin of Books By Design and Mary Sanger, the copyeditor. In addition I would like to thank Laura Kintz and Jennifer Jovin, editorial assistants on this project. My graduate assistants, Albert Ybarra and Nickoal Eichmann, also deserve thanks—I hope that they both enjoyed making the acquaintance of Champlain and his *Works*.

I am also grateful to the following instructors, who reviewed the manuscript and provided useful feedback: Leslie Choquette, Assumption

College; Christopher Hodson, Brigham Young University; Mary-Elle Kelm, Simon Fraser University; Elsa Nystrom, Kennesaw State University; and Eric Thierry, Centre de Recherche sur la Littérature des Voyages (Université de Paris–Sorbonne).

Gayle K. Brunelle

Contents

APPENDIXES

Maps and Illustrations

Samuel de Champlain: Founder of New France

A Brief History with Documents

PART ONE

Introduction: Samuel de Champlain— Between France and the New World

Samuel de Champlain is widely regarded as the "Founder of New France." In recent years historians have modified that assessment by pointing out that other French and Native American figures also played indispensable roles in establishing the French colony in North America. Still, Champlain was the driving force in the creation and survival of New France between 1613 and his death in 1635. Champlain's greatest contributions to the history of North America lie in his far-reaching exploration; in his persistent advocacy at the French court on behalf of New France; in his foundation in 1608 of the first permanent French settlement at Québec; in his extensive exploration and mapping of northeastern North America; in the alliances he strove to build and nurture between the Native peoples and the French; and especially in the works he authored recounting all of these things. These works shaped the perception of the history and meaning of New France from his day to the present. In his works we also find a meticulous observer of the natural and human worlds, a trait not surprising in a soldier who also possessed artistic talent and who excelled in cartography and navigation.[1] Through his books, and his constant lobbying of the French court, Champlain became the most forceful and tenacious supporter of the establishment of a permanent French colony in New France. Likewise, his vision of a

French colony whose economy was based on agriculture rather than the fur trade, a Catholic colony supporting vigorous evangelization of the Native peoples and controlling the water routes to the North American interior, ultimately became the vision of the French crown as well. There may have been a New France in the end without Champlain and his works, but it would have been a very different colony from the one Champlain established.

Champlain made twelve voyages to the New World between 1603 and 1633 and authored four volumes on his explorations and observations of the Natives and his activities as a trader, diplomat, and colonial administrator. None of his books enjoyed a wide readership in his own day, but they circulated among scholars, politicians, missionaries, and merchants interested in colonial affairs—men of influence who found his passionate defense of the French colonial enterprise persuasive and inspiring.[2] The primary purpose of Champlain's books was as propaganda in his tireless struggle to elicit support in France for exploring and colonizing North America. They are thus neither neutral nor scientific documents in the modern meaning of either word. Champlain wrote his narratives as a firsthand observer of the events he described, and they are clearly skewed by his cultural biases. Yet Champlain's straightforward, unembellished writing style sets his accounts apart from those of contemporaries who also voyaged to the New World and authored narratives of their adventures there; in comparison, Champlain's writing was remarkably objective and dispassionate, at times even rather dry.[3] His words are those of a man of action rather than of scholarly reflection, a military man who plunges into his narrative as if charging into battle. Much more than other explorers of his era who wrote about their travels, Champlain purposely attempted to maintain a narrative voice in which he, the narrator, appeared to be a witness observing events and a source of information even while recounting his own exploits.[4]

Besides comprising an invaluable historical narrative of the foundation of New France, Champlain's works are significant because they demonstrate a new, more dispassionate, observation-based approach to travel accounts. In addition, they contain invaluable data about the flora and fauna of North America and numerous images based on drawings and sketches Champlain made himself. Thus his works reflect a fundamental transition in European literature between the sixteenth and seventeenth centuries toward a more scientific approach to observing and writing about the New World. Perhaps of greatest importance, however, are the maps Champlain produced for these works.[5] Not only did they record succinctly and, for his era, quite accurately the results of his

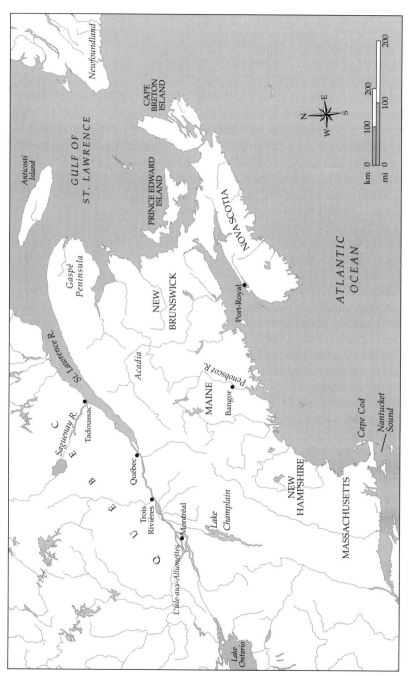

Map 1. *Region of Champlain's explorations, 1603–1607.*

3

explorations of territories previously unknown to France, but they laid the basis for Canadian cartography and played a central role in reshaping Europeans' understanding of North American geography. They remained unrivalled in their accuracy and quality until the second half of the seventeenth century, and no works on New France were more informative than Champlain's until the publication of the Jesuit *Relations* (beginning in 1632).[6]

Although Champlain never held the official title of "royal geographer" and never received formal scientific training, his works did reflect a technical and methodical approach to observing and recording information that was unusual among explorers of his day.[7] Champlain's contemporaries recognized the high quality of his maps and descriptions of the geography of the New World.[8] Champlain's maps and charts, and his commentaries on them and on mapmaking (Documents 4, 5, 6, and 7), are of signal importance to the history of geography because they provide one of the few opportunities scholars have to study a series of early maps in conjunction with written journals that detail the voyages during which the observations upon which the maps are based were made. This allows us to trace the evolution of Champlain's knowledge of the New World. Moreover, Champlain also took the time to explain the cartographic techniques he used in making his maps.[9] Despite some errors of projection and distance, Champlain's maps represent an enormous advance in mapmaking compared to preceding and contemporary maps of North America.[10]

When Champlain first arrived in New France in 1603, the French had no permanent settlement there, only a few trading posts where a motley collection of Basque and French seamen and fur traders came each year to purchase pelts from the Natives. Most of the Europeans who sailed to Acadia and the Saint Lawrence Valley were focused on the rich cod fishing off Newfoundland's Grand Banks and, increasingly, on obtaining furs, which were used in Europe for lining and decorating clothing and for making hats.[11] Champlain nurtured a vision of a self-sufficient New France founded solidly on the bedrock of agriculture. Geography, however, and economic interests in France conspired to ensure that French colonial ventures in Canada during Champlain's lifetime depended first and foremost on the fur trade.[12]

The interests of the fur traders were opposed to those of the colonizers and their missionary allies.[13] Fur traders gained their living by acting as brokers who dealt with Native tribes such as the Etchemins and Mi'kmaqs of Acadia and the Montagnais (Innu) and their allies living north of the Saint Lawrence. Neither these Native peoples nor French fur traders had much to gain from agricultural colonies. Nor did the French fur traders advocate encouraging the Natives to adopt a sedentary lifestyle modeled on that of France, a goal that Champlain and the Récollet (Reformed Franciscan) and Jesuit missionaries who came to New France cherished as the key to Christianizing the Natives. European fur traders feared that their Native trading partners would lose interest in the fur trade if the Natives took up agriculture, thus disrupting the supply of pelts. Champlain struggled constantly against what he viewed as the lack of vision and patriotism of the merchants and fur traders who opposed his efforts to establish colonies, and he complained often about these, in his view, shortsighted and self-centered men.[14]

The Montagnais and other peoples of the Saint Lawrence Valley were likewise determined to keep control of the trade routes to the interior. While the Montagnais did not oppose French colonies as long as they were centers of trade and located along the Saint Lawrence River and not in the interior, the price for their assistance was that Champlain had to agree to participate in their wars with the Iroquois.[15] Champlain's choice to cement the French alliance with the Saint Lawrence Natives by taking up arms against the Iroquois established a pattern of enmity between the French and the powerful Iroquois confederacy, the Five Nations, which was based in what is today upstate New York, an enmity that endured until the English conquest of New France in 1759.

Despite the shared interests between the Natives and the French, mutual misapprehension was rife, and it is clear that Champlain lacked deep understanding of Native culture—he was more adept at describing Native behavior and customs than at understanding their meaning.[16] Champlain sought to encourage the Natives to settle down and adopt European-style intensive agriculture. He brought missionaries to New France in the hopes of Christianizing them and advocated intermarriage between the French and Natives. Unlike most European explorers of the era, Champlain did not appear to view the Natives as physically or mentally inferior to the French and was convinced that the Natives could be Christianized and taught to live in the French manner.[17] When Champlain referred to the Natives as "savages," he meant that they were people not living in a civilized manner (the word, in both French and English, commonly meant "wild" as "in a state of nature"), but fully human nonetheless. Thus his use of words demonstrates not so much a racist view of the Natives as a culturally biased, ethnocentric one.[18]

The observations of Native life and society in Champlain's works make up an irreplaceable body of information about Native life in seventeenth-century North America.[19] However, one great drawback to all of Champlain's observations of and interactions with the Natives was his lack of language skills, and throughout his life he had to depend on translators to communicate with them. Most of his conversations with the Natives were mediated via interpreters, often Europeans who had been sent as adolescents to live among the Montagnais, Ottawa, or Huron peoples to create a corps of interpreters for the French. Other interpreters were Natives who had learned French. Unlike the Récollet and Jesuit missionaries, therefore, Champlain never mastered any Native language and never succeeded in conversing directly with any Native except in French. Thus in all the documents in which Champlain depicts himself talking with Natives, his communication with them was exclusively via an interpreter, even when that is not mentioned in the text.

FRANCE AND NORTH AMERICA BEFORE CHAMPLAIN

Although France is often considered to have been a relative latecomer in the European race to explore, colonize, and exploit the riches of the New World, French and Basque fishermen and fur traders reached the fishing grounds off the Grand Banks of Newfoundland very early—if not shortly before Columbus, then certainly by 1500.[20] Between 1524 and his death in 1547, French king Francis I sponsored three explorers of North America: Florentine navigator Giovanni da Verrazano, Saint-Malo pilot Jacques Cartier, and a Protestant member of the minor nobility, Jean-François de la Roque, Sieur de Roberval. The primary goal of their voyages was to search for a northern sea route through or around North America, the famed Northwest Passage. The discovery of such a route was especially attractive to the French because they could then reach the rich markets of Asia without having to sail through the Spanish-, Dutch-, or Portuguese-controlled waters of South America or Africa. Verrazano died in 1528 on the island of Guadeloupe, during his third voyage to the New World, without ever finding the much-coveted Northwest Passage.

When Cartier arrived in the Saint Lawrence Valley in 1534, the indigenous peoples that inhabited the northeastern section of North America belonged primarily to two main language groups that ethnologists call Algonquian and Iroquoian. Cartier initiated the first direct contact between Europeans and the Iroquoian-speaking peoples of the interior Saint Lawrence Valley. The Saint Lawrence Iroquoians and the Mi'kmaq inhabitants of Acadia initially greeted the French enthusiastically, although both Cartier and Roberval and their men soon managed to alienate the Natives. The hostility of the Saint Lawrence Iroquoians engendered by Cartier and Roberval helped to close off the region to French explorers for at least a generation. The failures of Cartier and Roberval to locate either a Northwest Passage or easily exploitable sources of gold and silver discouraged further royal initiatives to settle the region. Meanwhile, during the period from 1550 to 1603, momentous political and social upheavals were going on in both France and the Saint Lawrence Valley. The France of Champlain in 1603 was in some ways very different from the France of Cartier and on the cusp of even greater changes to come. This was also true of the Saint Lawrence Valley that Champlain encountered.

During the second half of the sixteenth century, France was engulfed in a series of bloody civil wars known as the Wars of Religion because they pitted French Protestants (Huguenots) against Catholics. The religious struggle lasted from 1562 until 1598 when the famous Edict of Nantes established a compromise both parties could accept, albeit reluctantly. It was a clash over religion, to be sure, but also over political power and in particular control of the French throne. In what French historians often term "the war of the three Henrys," three factions, each headed by a "Henri," vied for power: the ultra-Catholic League, controlled by Duke Henri de Guise; the more moderate Catholics, led until 1589 by the last Valois king Henri III; and the Huguenots, under the leadership of Henri de Bourbon, prince of Navarre. Henri III had Guise assassinated on December 23, 1588, and he himself was assassinated in August 1589—but only after having allied himself with Henri de Navarre and adopting Navarre as his heir, which precipitated a new phase of the wars. Only one Henri remained, and he was now legally the king of France, even though still a Protestant. Many moderate "royalist" Catholics rallied to Navarre's cause at that point, but the League and its Spanish allies fought on, and many other Catholics remained on the fence until Henri de Navarre, now Henri IV, finally converted to Catholicism in July 1593. France endured five more years of war, however, until internal peace was restored with the Edict of Nantes, and the Peace of Vervins was signed with Spain a month later in May 1598.[21]

The fallout of this decades-long struggle had repercussions for France's endeavors in the New World. After internal peace was restored in France under Henri IV, the exhausted French treasury possessed few resources to devote to his colonial projects. Henri IV therefore relied on granting royal monopolies over the fur trade to private entrepreneurs, often soldier-cronies who were loyal to him during the religious wars, in order to fund the establishment of French colonies. This system created numerous headaches for Champlain. The private merchants of French cities such as Rouen, Saint-Malo, and La Rochelle resisted submitting to the authority of the monopoly holders. In the period when Champlain was active in the New World, however, during the reigns of Henri IV and his successor, Louis XIII, the trend was clear. As the French crown succeeded in establishing its authority and centralizing its political control in France, it also became increasingly determined to dominate the territory France claimed in the New World, lending its support to Champlain and his successors and reining in the independence of the private merchants and monopoly holders.

Change was also under way in the Saint Lawrence Valley between 1500 and 1603, and it too was the result of political and economic conflict stemming from demographic shifts, as well as intertribal rivalries that predated the arrival of the Europeans. The burgeoning trade between Europeans and Native societies, and the influx into the interior via Native trade routes of European products, helped fuel these intertribal rivalries and shift the balance of power among peoples not always even in direct contact with Europeans. The most significant result of these changes, from the perspective of Champlain's career, was that by the time of his arrival in the Saint Lawrence Valley in 1603, the Iroquoian peoples that Cartier had encountered were gone, dispersed, and/or absorbed into other societies. It is easy to forget that Native societies were neither static nor timeless: Their history was as dynamic as that of Europeans, even though we may know less about it.

In Cartier's time, the Saint Lawrence Iroquois were at war with peoples from the Ottawa River Valley and the Mi'kmaq. Wars between Algonquian-speaking and Iroquoian-speaking peoples further west in the region of the Great Lakes and the Upper Susquehanna River led to migrations and conflicts over territory in the Saint Lawrence Valley as well. The Huron, also an Iroquoian-speaking people who inhabited the region between Lake Huron and Georgian Bay to the west, appear to have eliminated the Saint Lawrence Iroquois who controlled the territory between the Huron and the European trading outposts to the east.[22] When Champlain arrived in 1603, it was therefore the Mi'kmaq and the Montagnais who were the primary commercial partners of the French fur traders and now became the principal political allies of the French colonizers as well.

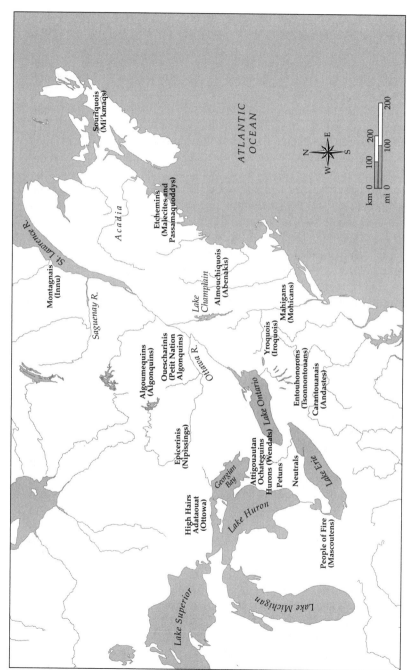

Map 2. Aboriginal nations in the regions Champlain explored.

9

CHAMPLAIN'S LIFE: EXPLORER, CARTOGRAPHER, DIPLOMAT, ENIGMA

We know remarkably little about Samuel de Champlain's private life. We lack a reliable portrait of him, although numerous bogus ones have been produced, and his writings reveal few biographical details and only inadvertent glimpses into his personality.[23] By the same token, Champlain's legacy has been subject to vigorous debate in recent decades. Thus, although the events that marked Champlain's life are clear, their meaning and significance are much less so.[24]

Among the many mysteries surrounding Champlain's biography is his exact date of birth, which most scholars place around 1570.[25] He was born in the town of Brouage, in the region of France known as Saintonge, on the west coast not far from the famous Protestant stronghold of La Rochelle. His parents were descendants of seafaring families, and his father, Anthoine, was a ship's pilot sufficiently prosperous to elevate his family into the upper levels of Brouage's middle class. Champlain therefore spent his youth around sailors and ship's pilots, and although his formal education ended well before the level of university, he received extensive training in navigation and sailing. Even though he was not a noble, Champlain acquired the skills necessary to be a soldier, including wielding a sword and riding a horse, training that commoners did not usually receive in early modern France. He also learned drawing and mapmaking, possibly from Charles Leber du Carlo, a royal engineer and skilled geographer and cartographer who lived in Brouage during Champlain's youth and was a family friend.[26]

Brouage had a large population of French Protestants at that time, and Champlain's first name suggests that he was baptized a Protestant, as does his subsequent marriage to a woman from a Protestant family of Paris. Still, by the time Champlain traveled to New France in 1603, like many Protestants he had evidently converted to Catholicism, although his devotion to that religion appears to have remained lukewarm until the 1620s.[27] The conversion of Henri IV to Catholicism in 1593 prompted many of his Protestant followers to convert as well. Champlain was probably among these converts.[28]

Around 1595 Champlain became a soldier in the royal army, now under the control of Henri IV, who was an important patron for Champlain. His years in the army from 1595 to 1598 were of seminal importance in Champlain's life both for the training he received during that period and for the connections he made that afforded him access to Henri IV and his court. The favor and intimacy Henri accorded Champlain, a commoner who was from a family neither noble nor particularly distinguished outside of their hometown of Brouage, has led some historians to speculate that Champlain was Henri's illegitimate son. Henri had several official mistresses and many more short-term dalliances and fathered multiple illegitimate children. Although no direct evidence exists to support this contention, there is no doubt that the two men developed a surprisingly strong connection that served Champlain well until Henri was assassinated in 1610.

A more likely reason for Henri's favor was that the young Champlain's talents became apparent to the king early on. We know that in 1595 Champlain received a bonus for having undertaken a "certain secret voyage in the king's service."[29] Although Champlain served in combat, his primary occupation was as a quartermaster, where he would have been expected to engage in military reconnaissance, draw up maps, and help to supply the royal army and locate lodgings for soldiers while they were on the march. His work as a quartermaster thus would have provided him with valuable experience in the sorts of logistical problems he later encountered while in charge of colonies in New France. And it is likely that he developed his remarkable cartographical skills through helping to prepare the maps that his superiors used to plot the resources available for the army in different regions of France.[30]

When the war ended in 1598, Champlain found himself at loose ends. His next move exemplifies his boldness and initiative: "Seeing myself thereby without any charge or employment, I resolved, so as not to remain idle, to find the means to make a voyage to Spain, and, there, to acquire and cultivate acquaintances, in order, by their favor and intermediary, to manage to embark in some one of the ships of the fleet which the king of Spain sends every year to the West Indies; to the end that I might be able there to make inquiries into particulars of which no Frenchmen have succeeded in obtaining cognizance, because they have no free access there, in order to make true report of them to his Majesty on my return."[31] Champlain essentially proposed to make himself a spy in the king's service. His goal was to find a means to travel to the Spanish territories in the New World, which were closed to non-Spanish travelers on pain of death unless they received special licenses from the Spanish crown. Champlain nevertheless managed to obtain permission to sail to the West Indies, territory that Spain jealously kept off limits to foreign interlopers and especially the French, their recent foes, through the good offices of his uncle, sea Captain Guillaume Allène, also known as the "Capitaine Provençal" because Allène hailed from Provence.

The Capitaine Provençal had served in the Spanish merchant marine and was on good terms with the Spanish government, which hired him to repatriate the Spanish soldiers garrisoned in a fort in Brittany known as Blavet (today Port Louis). When the fort and surrounding territory fell to the French at the end of the religious wars, the garrison, essentially stranded in France, needed to be evacuated from France to Spain. The Spanish government hired a ship, the *Saint-Julien*, of which Capitaine Provençal was also partial owner, to help transport the Spaniards. Champlain accompanied his uncle on the voyage to Cadiz in Spain as an observer and an unofficial aide-de-camp.

In Spain, the Capitaine Provençal received a new commission from the Spanish government directing him to sail to the Mediterranean. But the head of the Spanish treasure fleet that year, Don Francisco Coloma, decided to hire the *Saint-Julien* and her French crew to bolster the size of the Spanish flotilla. The Capitaine Provençal agreed to the deal but stipulated that Champlain must be permitted to accompany the treasure fleet in order to safeguard the *Saint-Julien*. Coloma agreed and Champlain sailed to the Spanish Indies with the fleet, which left Sanlúcar de Barrameda on February 3, 1599, and returned to Spain in August 1600.[32] Champlain did not return to French territory until the summer of 1601, in part because his uncle fell ill and died in Cadiz in June of that year.

At about this time Champlain began drafting a report detailing his experiences and observations while in the West Indies. This report is believed to have formed the basis for the *Brief Narrative of the Most Remarkable Things that Samuel de Champlain of Brouage Observed in the West Indies, 1599–1601* (manuscript c. 1601 and first published in 1859).[33] The *Brief Narrative* has long been controversial. Even though some aspects of it, such as the illustrations, the careful observations in many passages, and the accuracy of the maps, suggest that Champlain authored it, the *Brief Narrative* also is riddled with errors and inaccuracies that have led some historians to conclude that it is a forgery.[34] Therefore, although we know that Champlain kept a journal of his voyage to the West Indies and made a report to Henri IV when he returned to France, we do not know whether Champlain actually authored the *Brief Narrative* or if someone else subsequently used Champlain's unpublished notes as the foundation for the work.

It was again due to his own initiative that Champlain first traveled to the Saint Lawrence Valley and Acadia. While frequenting Henri IV's court in Paris during the winter of 1602–1603, Champlain heard from his contacts that Henri IV had placed Aymar de Chaste, vice admiral of the navy, in charge of sending an expedition to New France to found a colony. Champlain approached de Chaste and then the king and received permission to join the expedition as an unofficial observer enjoined once again to give the king a "faithful report" upon his return.[35] "So I am sent off," Champlain wrote, and on March 15, 1603, Champlain set sail on the *Bonne-Renommée* under the command of François Gravé, Sieur du Pont (usually known as Pont-Gravé), leader of the expedition.[36]

Their sojourn in New France was relatively brief; they were back in France by the end of the summer of 1603. But the consequences of the trip were enormous because soon after their arrival in New France, Pont-Gravé—with Champlain at his side—met with the leaders of the Montagnais people near Tadoussac, a trading post on the Saint Lawrence River near the mouth of the Saguenay River (Document 8). When Champlain and Pont-Gravé arrived at Tadoussac in 1603, the Montagnais leader, Anadabijou (probably a title rather than a name), was hosting a *tabagie* (feast) to celebrate the joint victory of the Montagnais, Algonquins, and Etchemins over their enemies, the Iroquois. This feast proved crucial because Anadabijou invited the Frenchmen to meet with him during the feast, at which time he offered to revive an alliance he had made with the French in 1600. This alliance between the Montagnais and the French endured for the entire history of New France and shaped that history because it bound the French to a system of alliances and conflicts among the Natives that predated the arrival of the French and over which the French had little control.[37] The Montagnais and their Algonquin allies were at war with the Iroquois living south of Lake Ontario and desired French help against them—help which Champlain was obliged to provide both to retain their support and to protect the fur trade along the Saint Lawrence River from Iroquois incursions. The Montagnais established themselves as intermediaries between the French and the tribes in the interior who—as the fur-bearing animals in the Saint Lawrence region became depleted due to overhunting—were increasingly the ones who actually obtained most of the pelts. Without the permission and support of the Saint Lawrence peoples, the French could not have successfully established colonies along the Saint Lawrence or dominated the fur trade in that region.[38]

When Champlain and Pont-Gravé returned to France in September 1603, they discovered that de Chaste had died. They advised Henri IV to transfer the vice admiralty of New France to another Huguenot veteran of the Wars of Religion and an old associate of Pont-Gravé, Pierre Dugua de Mons. Henri appointed de Mons vice admiral and also accorded him the title of lieutenant general for the king in New France.[39] In addition, Champlain and Pont-Gravé told Henri about silver and copper mines that a trader from Saint-Malo assured them, falsely, existed in Acadia. Pont-Gravé was particularly insistent that the French should focus their attention on Acadia, both to exploit the mines that they expected to find there and to take advantage of its milder climate, which seemed more conducive to an agricultural colony than that of the Lower Saint Lawrence River.

The king gave de Mons a monopoly on the fur trade between the latitudes of forty and forty-six degrees for a period of ten years in order to fund the establishment of colonies in Acadia.[40] The Basque fishermen and the merchants of the cities of Rouen, Saint-Malo, and La Rochelle—who had developed a thriving fur trade with the Natives without establishing settlements—did not appreciate losing out on the profits of that trade or being forced to subsidize colonies that they viewed as expensive and superfluous. They thus continually sought to undermine support for the monopolies at court and to circumvent and subvert them in New France. Clashes with these merchants became a major headache for Champlain throughout his career.[41]

During the autumn of 1603, even as he was busy lobbying the king and planning for his return to New France, Champlain found the time to write his first work on New France, *Of Savages, or Voyage of Samuel Champlain of Brouage, Made to New France in the Year 1603* (Documents 8 and 9). In April 1604 Champlain returned to New France with de Mons and Pont-Gravé, and with them sailed a nobleman from Picardy, Jean de Biencourt, Sieur de Poutrincourt,[42] who was interested in settling in Acadia and founding a colony there. Pont-Gravé remained in the Saint Lawrence region overseeing the annual cod-fishing fleet, while de Mons and Champlain sailed south to explore the coast of Acadia for potential settlement sites (Document 1). Because de Mons was well aware of the difficulties that French explorers and would-be colonizers during the sixteenth century had experienced trying to winter over in the harsh Canadian climate, he redirected the focus of his enterprise from the Saint Lawrence River to Acadia and the coast of what was then called Norumbega, today's Maine.[43] After they had explored the coast as far south as Muscongus Bay, Maine, the arrival of autumn forced Champlain and his crew to return to Acadia. They decided to winter on an island in the Saint Croix River, known today as Saint Croix Island (Maine/New Brunswick), and send Poutrincourt back to France with a rich cargo of furs for the shareholders in the monopoly.

De Mons and Champlain made grave errors in choosing to pass the winter in Saint Croix. They selected the island during fine weather, prior to having experienced a Canadian winter, which was much harsher than those they knew in France. More interested in finding a site that was easily defensible than one that offered shelter from the elements and a good source of running water, they did not take into account that the river would freeze during the winter and become filled with dangerous ice floes that prevented crossing it. Nor did they realize that the nearly treeless island would offer them few opportunities to hunt fresh game, little in the way of firewood, and no shelter from the howling winter winds. The winter of 1604 on Saint Croix Island turned out to be much harsher than Champlain or de Mons had expected, and thirty-six of the seventy-nine men in the tiny settlement died, mostly of scurvy. Only eleven of the survivors, among them Champlain, were in good health.

After experiencing this disastrous winter at Saint Croix Island, Champlain decided that the Upper Saint Lawrence region would offer a better location to establish a colony. Champlain was unable to convince de Mons of the superiority of the Upper Saint Lawrence for several years, however, and therefore continued exploring Acadia. He and Poutrincourt spent the winter of 1605 at a new site in Acadia, Port-Royal (now Annapolis Royal in Nova Scotia). This winter at Port-Royal, while less deadly than the preceding one at Saint Croix, still took a serious toll in illness and mortality on the already small colony. De Mons, prior to returning to France in September 1605 to deal with political challenges from the French merchants to his monopoly, ordered Champlain and Poutrincourt again to reconnoiter the Atlantic coast. They explored much of the Maine coastline and the Penobscot River in 1605 and 1606 and made contact with the Malecite people inhabiting that region. They had more difficulty in establishing friendly relations with the peoples living south of the Penobscot. Members of an Algonquian tribe the French knew as the Almouchiquois ambushed some of the French near Cape Cod, after the French had attempted alternately to trade with, and bully, the Natives. The French returned to Port-Royal in the autumn of 1606 having accomplished little beyond exploration, only to discover that de Mons, under pressure from rival French merchants and the Dutch, had gone bankrupt and dissolved the company. Because by that point it was too late in the season to return to France in accordance with de Mons's orders, they had to spend another winter at Port-Royal.[44]

During that winter at Port-Royal, 1606–1607, Champlain created the "Order of Good Cheer," a kind of fraternity in which members took turns hunting and preparing a feast each evening for each other and their Native guests (Document 13). The evenings featured entertainment, including speeches, dancing, and smoking tobacco, a custom adopted from the Natives.[45] Mortality and serious illness were both low compared to the previous winter. But upon returning to France in the spring of 1607, Champlain was dismayed to discover that the hostility of the merchants to the colonial venture had prevailed. Responding to the merchants' complaints, the king had rescinded de Mons's monopoly on the fur trade in New France, which jeopardized the future of the colony.

In January 1608 de Mons, whose tenacity and devotion to New France were central to the success of French colonization there, managed to persuade Henri IV to renew his monopoly, albeit for a single year. Hoping to make the most of this small concession, de Mons sent Pont-Gravé and Champlain, whom he had now officially appointed his lieutenant, back to New France in April 1608. Champlain had finally convinced de Mons to allow him to try to establish a settlement along the Saint Lawrence River. De Mons conceded Acadia to Poutrincourt, who reestablished the settlement at Port-Royal that de Mons had originally founded in 1605. Champlain, by contrast, concentrated for the rest of his life on the Saint Lawrence and its watershed, the rivers that linked it northward to Hudson's Bay, westward to the Great Lakes region, and southward to Lake Champlain, which Champlain reached during the summer of 1609. Champlain was the first European to reach Lake Champlain, which straddles the border of present-day New York and Vermont and which he named after himself. The year 1608 began the second, and final, phase of Champlain's career as an explorer.[46]

During the years 1608–1618, Champlain made no fewer than seven trips to New France as he divided his time between his activities in the New World and lobbying the French court. While in Paris in December 1610, Champlain—then near forty years of age—signed a marriage contract with the parents of twelve-year-old Hélène Boullé. Although the couple was legally married, it was stipulated that the marriage was not to be consummated for another two years. Champlain and his wife seem not to have developed a close relationship during their marriage, which is unsurprising given the difference in their ages. Still, the marriage brought Champlain important financial benefits. Moreover, he became close to Hélène's younger brother Eustache, who sailed with him to New France in 1618. Hélène went with Champlain to Québec in 1620, where she resided with him and her brother for four years, but the couple remained childless and spent much of the marriage apart. Both Hélène and Eustache were devout Catholics despite their Protestant background (after Champlain's death Hélène became an Ursuline nun and Eustache entered the priesthood).[47] Champlain also became more religious during the years after 1615, perhaps in recognition of the growing Catholic piety at the French court that could garner him patrons among wealthy nobles who wished to sponsor missions to the Natives. In 1615 Champlain brought four Récollet missionaries to New France.

COLONIAL ADMINISTRATOR

On July 3, 1608, Champlain founded the colony of Québec. He chose the site because it was located on a narrowing of the Saint Lawrence River (its name most likely derives from a Mi'kmaq word for "strait") that strategically permitted French guns from a fort built on the highland to command the river but was below the formidable rapids at Lachine, thus facilitating trade with the Natives. Québec was also located in a region where the soil and climate were more favorable to the self-sufficient agricultural colony Champlain hoped would spring up there.

Champlain had to make the trek back to France almost every year from 1608 through 1618 because he was forced to shoulder a growing share of the burden of lobbying the court to support the fledgling colony. Even so, Champlain found time to become deeply involved in Native conflicts in order to fulfill the terms of the treaty the French had made with them in 1603 and thus retain their respect and support. The Montagnais and their Algonquin allies also refused to assist Champlain in exploring the Ottawa River or the territory between the Ottawa and Lake Huron until he had demonstrated his fidelity to them by participating in their conflicts with the Iroquoian peoples who controlled the southern banks of the Saint Lawrence River. Thus, in June and July 1609, Champlain traveled into Iroquois territory as far south as Lake Champlain. At the site of the future Fort Ticonderoga (in what is now Crown Point, New York), Champlain and two other Frenchmen joined their Native allies in battles with a band of Mohawks, in which (according to Champlain's account) French firearms and Champlain's courage and skill played a decisive role (Document 11).[48] The following summer Champlain again joined his Native allies in a second confrontation with the Iroquois, again a victory for the French and their allies.

Champlain's hope was that by defeating the Iroquois soundly in their own territory he could stem their raids on his Native allies, raids that were also a threat to French settlements and the fur trade. His policy seems to have worked fairly well, for from that year until 1640 the Iroquois largely avoided raiding French territory in the Saint Lawrence Valley and for a time even made a fragile peace with the French. But

Champlain's primary motivation for partaking in these battles was his realization that only by establishing his credentials as a true ally — which for the Natives meant being willing to fight alongside them against their enemies — could he obtain the permission and guides, albeit grudgingly offered, that he needed to further his explorations.[49] Thus it was only after his first two battles with the Iroquois that in 1613 Champlain succeeded in exploring the Ottawa Valley from Sault Saint-Louis to the Île aux Allumettes (Morrison Island, Ontario) (Document 2). Similarly, in order to obtain guides to Huronia and permission to visit the neighboring Nipissing people of the Lake Nipissing region, which he accomplished during the summer of 1615, Champlain assured his Montagnais and Algonquin allies that his goal in making these visits was to cement an alliance to help them fight their enemies. He kept this promise, joining his Native allies for a third and final battle against the Iroquois in October 1615 (Document 12). Exploring the North American interior remained in this period a central goal for Champlain, as neither he nor the French crown had relinquished the dream of discovering a Northwest Passage to Asia.

During this period, Champlain also had to contend with political upheavals back in France. The assassination of Henri IV in 1610 was a traumatic event for Champlain. Not only did he lose his royal mentor, who had been supportive of the New France venture, but he also lost his patron and employer, Dugua de Mons, who was no longer in favor with the crown. Queen Mother Marie de Medici, who ruled on behalf of the young Louis XIII until he came of age, was a weak ruler with few resources to spare for New France. Moreover, as a Huguenot, de Mons found his influence at court greatly diminished under Marie de Medici, who was less favorable to Protestants than her convert husband had been. Champlain thus found himself obliged to find a new patron for the colony and, on the advice of influential friends at court, decided to seek one who was not only Catholic but of a much higher station than de Mons. In 1612 he found such a patron in a cousin of Louis XIII, Charles de Bourbon, Comte de Soissons, who appointed Champlain his lieutenant at the settlement at Québec. When Soissons died suddenly in November 1612, the Prince de Condé, also a Bourbon cousin of Louis XIII, was appointed viceroy of New France in Soissons's stead. Condé kept Champlain on as his lieutenant general.

Freedom of trade was turning out to be less profitable than the merchants had hoped. The hordes of rapacious Frenchmen descending upon the Saint Lawrence Valley each year created rising tensions as the traders vied with each other for the Natives' furs. This situation reinforced Champlain's conviction that the survival of both the fur trade and his colony at Québec depended on the revival of the monopoly. Fortunately, the raid of the English Captain Samuel Argall on Acadia in July 1613 convinced the crown and the viceroy that action to preserve their colonies in New France was needed, and in November they obliged merchants trading along the Saint Lawrence River to join a new monopoly company, the Canada Company. Not surprisingly, 1613 was also the year Champlain published his second important work on New France, *The Voyages of the Sieur de Champlain of Saintonge, Captain in the Ordinary for the King in the Navy* (1613) and the *Fourth Voyage of the Sieur de Champlain, Captain in Ordinary for the King in the Navy* (1613) (Documents 1, 6, 10, and 11), which were published together in a single volume and detailed his activities from 1604 through 1613.[50]

The years 1608–1618 also marked the period in which Champlain laid the foundations of the alliances and enmities between the French and the Natives of northeastern North America that persisted until France ceded its North American possessions to the British in the 1763 Treaty of Paris and to the fledgling United States in the 1803 Louisiana Purchase. Champlain desperately wanted to explore the region between the Saint Lawrence River and the Great Lakes about which the Natives had informed him. He also sought to build a relationship with the Natives of the interior, such as the Huron, Neutrals, and Ottawa, who were increasingly becoming the primary producers of the furs that the French obtained from trading posts along the Saint Lawrence. Champlain was not in control of the relationship between the French and the Natives, however, and he knew it, although he worked hard to establish himself as an indispensable mediator among them.[51] Champlain's last great voyage of exploration into the North American interior ended in the spring of 1616.

The year 1618 marked an important turning point in the history of New France and in Champlain's career, as his focus shifted from exploration and observation toward lobbying for and administering the colony he had founded at Québec. In February Champlain wrote memoranda to the king and the royal council and to the Paris Chamber of Commerce in which he enumerated the many advantages he was certain France would accrue from colonizing the Saint Lawrence region and the lamentable record so far of the private monopoly companies in achieving this.[52] He also penned his third work on New France at this time, his *Voyages and Discoveries Made in New France, from the Year 1615 until the End of the Year 1618* (1619) (Document 12), again to help drum up public support for colonization.

To this point only one family of French colonists had settled in the Saint Lawrence Valley.[53] Champlain's frustration was evident in his memoranda, as he laid out his own colonial project that with sufficient crown support and private and public funds would enable him to succeed where the companies so far had failed in creating a viable, self-sustaining French colony in New France. With the support of the Paris Chamber of Commerce, Champlain convinced the king, who ordered the company directors to assist Champlain in his role as lieutenant of the king's viceroy, Condé, in achieving the goal of settling at least three hundred French families per year in New France. Champlain spent the summer of 1618 in New France, taking with him his eighteen-year-old brother-in-law Eustache Boullé.[54] He continued to meet determined resistance from the merchant directors of the company upon his return to France in the fall, and that opposition persisted into 1619 when they refused to permit him to board their ship leaving for New France that spring. But on February 25, 1620, the king again confirmed Champlain's command of New France as lieutenant of the viceroy (now the duke of Montmorency, who had purchased the office from Condé), leaving the monopoly company's merchants in charge only of the fishing and fur trading. Champlain was to administer the forts and settlements in the name of the viceroy and the king.

In 1620 Champlain made his tenth departure for New France, and this time his wife and household servants accompanied him.[55] They remained there for four years until their return to France in August 1624. These years were trying ones for Champlain. Montmorency had created a new monopoly company headed by Huguenot merchant Guillaume de Caën. The shareholders of the old monopoly company refused to accept the new company and sent Champlain's old friend Pont-Gravé to New France to trade for furs while the rights of the two companies were litigated before the Parlement of Paris and the royal council. Champlain's skills as a diplomat were sorely tried as he struggled to maintain the peace between Caën and Pont-Gravé, while also trying to negotiate a peace treaty between his Native allies and their enemies, the Iroquois (Document 15). By his return to France in 1624, however, things seemed to be looking up. A fragile peace between the Iroquois and the Native allies seemed to be holding. Moreover, the two rival companies had been merged peacefully into one under the leadership of both the Protestant merchant Guillaume de Caën and his Catholic cousin Émery de Caën, which made the new unified company more acceptable to Champlain and the mostly Catholic settlers in Québec. In addition, the Récollets had constructed their first church and opened a seminary in New France in 1620 (and brewed the first batch of beer ever made in New France), and a small group of new families had settled at Québec, although the colony's population, at barely a hundred, was still quite small compared to that of the English or the Dutch in North America.

In 1625 yet another new viceroy, Henri de Lévis, duke of Ventadour, took control of New France. Champlain's efforts seemed to have been appreciated, as Ventadour again confirmed Champlain as his lieutenant, with Eustache Boullé as Champlain's second-in-command. Ventadour took much more seriously than his predecessors the missionary obligations of the colony. Since the Récollets proved to be too small and poor an order to establish the number of missions necessary to convert the Natives in so vast a territory, Ventadour decided to sponsor their rivals, the Jesuits. The Jesuits opened their first monastery in New France in 1625. Although it was Champlain, along with Louis Houël, Sieur de Petit-Pré, who had first recruited the Récollets to work as missionaries in New France in 1615, by 1625 Champlain too had accepted that they were not up to the task. His own Catholic piety was growing in these years, and he and the Jesuits maintained cordial relations that strengthened during the ensuing decade. In 1626 Cardinal Richelieu, chief minister to Louis XIII, created and assumed the office of grand master, chief, and general superintendent of navigation and trade for France, and in 1627 Richelieu removed Ventadour as viceroy and took direct control of New France himself. He created a new monopoly company, the Company of New France (also known as the Company of the One Hundred Associates).

Trade was prospering and all seemed to be going well in New France in 1628, but trouble was on the horizon. In 1625 war had broken out between England and France, and English king Charles I had given his support to Anglo-Scottish merchants and adventurers seeking to wrest control of the fur trade and carve out English colonies in Acadia and the Saint Lawrence Valley. Among them were Jarvis Kirke and his sons, English merchants who had lived many years in Dieppe before returning to England. The Kirkes successfully lobbied the English crown for permission to expel the French from the Saint Lawrence Valley and reserve the profits of the fur trade for themselves. Thus, to Champlain's consternation, in 1628 the Kirkes intercepted the French fleet—which was bringing badly needed supplies to Québec—and blockaded the Saint Lawrence River (Document 16). Champlain held out for another winter and spring, but when July 1629 brought no aid or supplies from France, Champlain was forced to surrender Québec to Thomas Kirke. Ironically, Richelieu had officially appointed Champlain commander of

New France the preceding March. Moreover, unbeknownst to either Champlain or Thomas Kirke, the April 1629 Treaty of Susa had officially ended the conflict between the French and English, making the English seizure of Québec in July illegal. The Kirkes transported the French colonists to England and then permitted most of them to return to France, while the English remaining in the Saint Lawrence Valley worked feverishly to profit from the fur trade before the English and French crowns negotiated the return of Québec to the French.

There is little doubt that administration was not Champlain's strongest point, and some contemporaries (and some later historians) faulted Champlain for inadequately provisioning Québec to secure it against an English siege.[56] Nevertheless, Champlain was the only person between 1613 and 1633 who was willing and able to lobby consistently and effectively for the colony and to risk his life repeatedly in the New World and his wealth and reputation in France on its behalf. De Mons was the primary figure in this effort prior to 1613, but after that date it was left to Champlain to keep the dream alive. He managed to keep the colony functioning during extremely difficult times and often with only very weak support from France and in the face of much opposition both at court and in New France. The English conquest of Québec marked the nadir of Champlain's career and deprived him of his hard-won position of leadership. His resolve never wavered, however, and once the English released him, he hurried back to France, determined to do all in his power to prod the French crown into pressuring the English to relinquish the colony.

Champlain was never accorded the title of governor of New France even though as the lieutenant of various viceroys he carried out the work of a governor from at least 1618 on. Given the resistance he encountered in France and in the New World and the need to keep the peace between Catholic and Protestant factions in the settlement, as well as between the settlement and the Native allies, both of whom were often at odds among themselves, it is not surprising that Champlain sought consensus whenever possible. He lacked the military force and political authority to impose his will, and it is likely that a more authoritarian style would only have rendered more difficult the task of controlling the unruly, independent French traders, soldiers, and colonists in New France.[57] These divisions among the French weakened the colony fatally, especially as it was French fur traders who, unhappy with Champlain and with the whole colonial enterprise, assisted the English in capturing the supplies and reinforcements sent from France to aid Québec in 1628–1629.

It was not until March 1632 that the Treaty of Saint-Germain-en-Laye finally brought the return of Québec to the French, and it was only in March 1633 that Champlain, reappointed commander of New France, returned to Québec. While in France Champlain profited from the extra time to publish his final works, *Voyages to Western New France, Called Canada* (republished in 1830 as *The Voyages of Samuel de Champlain* and the *Treatise on Seamanship and the Duty of a Good Seaman*) (Document 7), which appeared together in 1632 with *The Voyages* (1632) (Documents 15 and 16). Champlain completed his twelfth and final crossing to New France in May 1633 and spent the following two years working on consolidating and expanding the French colony and strengthening its alliance with the Huron. By mid-1635 Champlain's health began to decline, and in October he became paralyzed, probably as the result of a stroke. On Christmas Day, 1635, with his close friend the Jesuit Charles Lalemant at his bedside, Champlain died.

CHAMPLAIN'S LEGACY: FOUNDER OF NEW FRANCE?

Champlain was by no means the sole founder of New France. He must share that honor with at least two other men, de Mons and Pont-Gravé, who were his superiors until 1618. De Mons in particular dedicated much of his fortune and many years of his life to trying to found a colony first in Acadia and then in the Saint Lawrence Valley, and without his tenacious efforts the Québec colony could not have survived. To this list should be added Anadabijou, the chief leader of the Montagnais who sealed the alliance with the French in 1603. Without his support and that of his fellow Natives gathered at Tadoussac that fateful summer, the French colony could never have been founded or have survived.

Nor did Champlain's career begin and end with New France. Champlain also blazed the path for French penetration much further west, to the Great Lakes, Hudson Bay, and ultimately the Mississippi River, through both his own explorations and the relationships with the Natives that he helped foster. The Natives always held the key to both the fur trade and penetration into the interior, and Champlain knew this. The good relations he sought to foster with them were meant to serve primarily the interests of a French empire in North America. But without Native cooperation, which the Natives accorded because they felt that it was in their own interests, European expansion into the interior of northern North America—and in the early decades that meant primarily French expansion—would have been a much slower and much bloodier affair. Champlain was no benign pacifist, but his realism regarding the need for Native alliances to achieve his dream of building a French colonial empire in North America helped to establish a very different type of relationship between the French and the Native peoples than that which developed further south in the English colonies. This, too, shaped the history of both Canada and the United States, as many of the southern Natives developed alliances with the English and the Dutch and thus became involved in colonial wars pitting the English colonists against the French and their Native allies to the north. Champlain's actions helped to set the stage for these alignments and for the conflicts involving both Europeans and Native peoples in northeastern North America in the seventeenth and eighteenth centuries.

But, historically, Champlain has always been remembered as the central figure in the foundation of New France. One reason for this is simply that it was Champlain who wrote about his explorations and adventures in New France. His works, while limited in circulation in his own time, impressed his exploits upon the minds of his contemporaries and of future generations, especially in the second half of the nineteenth century when interest in him revived in France, Canada, and the United States. For better or worse, it was primarily through his words that readers in his own day and since have learned about the founding of New France.

The passion with which Champlain regarded New France—as a place, but even more as a colonial project and an idea—is evident less in his rhetoric than in his career and in particular in the tenacity with which he pursued his dream of a New France in the face of physical hardships and almost constant conflict with his fellow Europeans. Champlain began his career in New France in 1603 as a simple observer without a particularly important official position. He served under a series of other royal lieutenants and viceroys as he worked to realize his dream of creating an enduring French colony based in the Upper Saint Lawrence Valley. For most of his career he had to share authority in New France with other men, Native and French alike, and he spent much of his time and energy as an administrator and as a mediator between Natives and the French, between fur traders and settlers, and between merchant shareholders and courtiers in France. His persistent advocacy in both Canada and France on behalf of the fledgling colony of Québec upon which he had pinned his hopes eventually won the confidence of Louis XIII and, more importantly, of Louis's chief minister, Cardinal Richelieu, who in 1629 finally placed Champlain in charge of New France. By the time of his death Champlain had created a solid foundation for a French colonial empire in Canada that lasted until 1763. Through his words and deeds he thus secured for himself a durable legacy as the "founder" of New France.

NOTES

[1] Maurice Lemire, "Champlain: entre l'objectivité et la subjectivité," in *Scritti sulla Nouvelle-France nel seicento. Quaderni del seicento francese*, no. 6 (Bari: Adriatica, 1984; Paris: Nizet, 1984), 42–57. For Champlain's training in painting and cartography, see David Buisseret, "The Cartographic Technique of Samuel de Champlain," *Imago Mundi* 61, no. 2 (June 2009): 256–59; François-Marc Gagnon, "Champlain: Painter?" in *Champlain: The Birth of French America*, ed. Raymonde Litalien and Denis Vaugeois, trans. Käthe Roth (Montréal: McGill-Queen's University Press, 2004), 302–11; Conrad E. Heidenreich and Edward H. Dahl, "Samuel de Champlain's Cartography, 1603–32," in Litalien and Vaugeois, *Champlain: The Birth of French America*, 312–32; Éric Thierry, "Introduction," in Samuel de Champlain, *Les foundations de l'Acadie et de Québec 1604–1611*, ed. Éric Thierry (Québec: Les Éditions du Septentrion, 2008), 14–15.

[2] Raymonde Litalien, "Historiography of Samuel Champlain," in Litalien and Vaugeois, *Champlain: The Birth of French America*, 12. See also Jean Glénisson and Raymonde Litalien, "Champlain's Voyage Accounts," in Litalien and Vaugeois, *Champlain: The Birth of French America*, 279–83; and Pierre Berthiaume, "From Champlain's Voyage Accounts to His 1632 Report," in Litalien and Vaugeois, *Champlain: The Birth of French America*, 284–301.

[3] Marc Lescarbot, *The History of New France*, ed. W. L. Grant, vol. 2 (Toronto: Champlain Society, 1911), 168–72. For Champlain's remark regarding Lescarbot's travels, see Champlain, *The Voyages* (1613), vol. 1, *The Works of Samuel de Champlain*, ed. Henry Percival Biggar et al. (Toronto: Champlain Society, 1922–1935; University of Toronto Press, 1971), 452. See also René Baudry, "Marc Lescarbot," in *Dictionary of Canadian Biography*, vol. 1, 1000 to 1700 (Toronto: University of Toronto Press, 1966), 469–72; David Hackett Fischer, *Champlain's Dream* (New York: Simon & Schuster, 2008), 207–8, 533–34; Frank Lestringant, "Champlain, Lescarbot et la 'Conference' des Histoires," in Lemire, *Scritti sulla Nouvelle-France nel seicento*, 69–112; Maurice K. Séguin, *Samuel de Champlain: L'entrepreneur et le rêveur* (Sillery, Québec: Les Éditions du Septentrion, 2008); Éric Thierry, "Champlain and Lescarbot: An Impossible Friendship," in Litalien and Vaugeois, *Champlain: The Birth of French America*, 121–34; Éric Thierry, *Marc Lescarbot (vers 1570–1641): Un homme de plume au service de la Nouvelle-France* (Paris: Honoré Champion Éditeur, 2001), 98, 302–4.

[4] Michel Bideaux, "*Des sauvages*: une singularité narrative," *Études françaises* 22, no. 2 (1986): 35–36.

[5] Raymonde Litalien, Jean-François Palomino, and Denis Vaugeois, *Mapping a Continent: Historical Atlas of North America 1492–1814*, trans. Käthe Roth (Québec: Les Éditions du Septentrion/McGill-Queen's University Press, 2007), 87–88; the most useful work on Champlain's cartographic skills and accomplishments is Conrad E. Heidenreich, *Explorations and Mapping of Samuel de Champlain 1603–1632*, monograph no. 17, *Cartographica* (1976).

[6] The Jesuit *Relations* were a series of letters that Jesuit missionaries wrote to their superiors in France beginning in 1611. The first of these letters were initially published in 1632, primarily because the Jesuits realized that the considerable general interest in them would make them useful propaganda for the Jesuit missions. They continued to be published yearly during the subsequent two hundred years. They are an invaluable source of information regarding Native American peoples in North America. Reuben Gold Thwaites, ed., *Quebec: 1632–1633*, vol. 5, *The Jesuit Relations and Allied Documents:*

Travels and Explorations of the Jesuit Missionaries in New France 1610–1791 (New York: Pageant Book Company, 1959), 199–203; Thwaites, *Quebec 1636*, vol. 9, *Jesuit Relations and Allied Documents*, 207–9; Dominique Deslandres, "Samuel de Champlain and Religion," in Litalien and Vaugeois, *Champlain: The Birth of French America*, 201–2; Caroline Galland, "L'Administration du spirituel par l'établissement des missions: Champlain, les Récollets et la Nouvelle-France 1613–1615," in Annie Blondel-Loisel and Raymonde Litalien, with Jean-Paul Barbiche and Claude Briot, *De la Seine au Saint-Laurent avec Champlain* (Paris: L'Harmattan, 2005), 159–219; Hackett Fischer, *Champlain's Dream*, 452–53.

    7 Litalien, Palomino, and Vaugeois, *Mapping a Continent*, 88.

    8 Christian Morissonneau, "Champlain's Place Names," in Litalien and Vaugeois, *Champlain: The Birth of French America*, 218; Éric Thierry, *Marc Lescarbot (vers 1570–1641)*, 305–6.

    9 Heidenreich, *Explorations and Mapping of Samuel de Champlain*, xii.

    10 Ibid., 98.

    11 The best study of the Canadian fur trade is Bernard Allaire, *Pelleteries, manchons et chapeaux de castor: les fourrures nord-américaines à Paris, 1500–1632* (Sillery, Québec: Les Éditions du Septentrion, 1999; Paris: Presses de l'Université de Paris-Sorbonne, 1999). See also Bernard Allaire, "The European Fur Trade and the Context of Champlain's Arrival," in Litalien and Vaugeois, *Champlain: The Birth of French America*, 50–59; Harold A. Innis, *The Fur Trade in Canada: An Introduction to Canadian Economic History*, rev. ed. (New Haven, Conn.: Yale University Press, 1962), 3–22.

    12 Sara E. Melzer, "The French *Relation* and Its 'Hidden' Colonial History," in *A Companion to the Literatures of Colonial America*, ed. Susan Castillo and Ivy Schweitzer (Malden, Mass.: Blackwell Publications, 2005), 232; Bruce G. Trigger, "The French Presence in Huronia: The Structure of Franco-Huron Relations in the First Half of the Seventeenth Century," *Canadian Historical Review* 49, no. 2 (June 1968): 121.

    13 Gayle K. Brunelle, *The New World Merchants of Rouen, 1559–1630*, Sixteenth Century Essays and Studies, vol. 16 (Kirksville, Mo.: Sixteenth Century Journal Publishers, 1991), 34–38; Marcel Trudel, *Le Comptoir*, vol. 2, *Histoire de la Nouvelle-France* (Montréal: Fides, 1966), 14–15.

    14 Samuel de Champlain, *The Voyages* (1619), in Biggar et al., *Works*, vol. 3, 205–6, and Samuel de Champlain, *The Voyages* (1632), part 2, in Biggar et al., *Works*, vol. 5, 3–4, 17–20.

    15 Conrad E. Heidenreich, "The Beginning of French Exploration Out of the Saint Lawrence Valley: Motives, Methods, and Changing Attitudes towards Native Peoples," in *Decentring the Renaissance: Canada and Europe in Multidisciplinary Perspective, 1500–1700*, ed. Germaine Warkentin and Carolyn Podruchny (Toronto: University of Toronto Press, 2001), 241–45; Trigger, "The French Presence in Huronia," 115–23; Bruce G. Trigger, *Natives and Newcomers: Canada's "Heroic Age" Reconsidered* (Kingston: McGill-Queen's University Press, 1985), 172–75.

    16 One of the best studies of this issue is Cornelius J. Jaenen, *Friend and Foe: Aspects of French-Amerindian Cultural Contact in the Sixteenth and Seventeenth Centuries* (New York: Columbia University Press, 1976). See also Bruce G. Trigger, "Champlain Judged by His Native Policy: A Different View of Early Canadian History," *Anthropologica* 13 (1971): 85–114; Hackett Fischer, *Champlain's Dream*, 334–36; Elisabeth Tooker, *An Ethnography of the Huron Natives, 1615–1649* (Washington, D.C.: U.S. Government Printing Office, 1964), 5–7.

    17 Samuel de Champlain, *Les Voyages* (1613), in Biggar et al., *Works*, vol. 2, 195–96, and Samuel de Champlain, *Voyages and Discoveries Made in New France* (1619), in Biggar et al., *Works*, vol. 3, 15–16; Hackett Fischer, *Champlain's Dream*, 142–45, 339–42; Jaenen, *Friend and Foe*, 153–56; Melzer, "The French *Relation*," 227, 229.

    18 For an excellent discussion of this issue and of the early modern tendency to use the term *savage* to describe Native Americans, see Thomas G. M. Peace,

"Deconstructing the Sauvage/Savage in the Writing of Samuel de Champlain and Captain John Smith," *French Colonial History* 7 (2006): 1–20.

[19] Tooker, *An Ethnography of the Huron Natives*, 3.

[20] The best introduction in English to the history of the French exploration of North America prior to Champlain remains Marcel Trudel's *The Beginnings of New France, 1524–1663* (Toronto: McClelland & Stewart, 1973). See also John L. Allen, "From Cabot to Cartier: The Early Exploration of Eastern North America, 1497–1543," *Annals of the Association of American Geographers* 82, no. 3 (September 1992): 500–521; Conrad E. Heidenreich and K. Janet Ritch, eds., *Samuel de Champlain Before 1604: Des Sauvages and Other Documents Related to the Period* (Toronto: Champlain Society, 2010), especially the introductory essay, "Champlain and His Times to 1604: An Interpretive Essay," 3–82.

[21] The best book for students and general readers regarding the French Wars of Religion is Mack P. Holt, *The French Wars of Religion, 1562–1669*, 2nd ed., New Approaches to European History (Cambridge, U.K.: Cambridge University Press, 2005).

[22] Marcel Moussette, "A Universe Under Strain: Amerindian Nations in North-eastern North America in the 16th Century," *Post-Medieval Archaeology* 43, no. 1 (2009): 41–42.

[23] The most famous portrait of Champlain is a fraud painted in 1854 by Louis-César Joseph Ducornet and based on the portrait of Michel Particelli d'Emery, the superintendant of finances under Louis XIII and Louis XIV. Hackett Fischer, *Champlain's Dream*, 1–4; Denis Martin, "Discovering the Face of Samuel de Champlain," in Litalien and Vaugeois, *Champlain: The Birth of French America*, 362; Marcel Trudel, "La carte de Champlain en 1632: Ses sources et son originalité," *Cartologica* 51 (July–December 1978): 19–20. Much of what we know about Champlain's life comes from documents scholars have unearthed from local archives since the nineteenth century, many of which Robert Le Blant and René Baudry published in 1967. Robert Le Blant and René Baudry, eds., *Nouveaux documents sur Champlain et son époque* (Ottawa: Archives Publiques du Canada, 1967).

[24] For summaries of scholarly treatments of Champlain's life and legacy, see Matthieu D'Avignon, *Champlain et les fondateurs oubliés: Les figures du père et le mythe de la fondation* (Québec: Les Presses de l'Université Laval, 2008); Patrice Groulx, "In the Shoes of Samuel de Champlain," in Litalien and Vaugeois, *Champlain: The Birth of French America*, 335–46; Hackett Fischer, *Champlain's Dream*, 533–67; Raymond Litalien, "Samuel Champlain, fondateur du Canada, sa présence dans la mémoire," in *Le Nouveau Monde et Champlain*, ed. Guy Martinière and Didier Poton (Paris: Les Indes Savantes, 2008), 17–26; and Raymond Litalien, "Historiography of Samuel Champlain," in Litalien and Vaugeois, *Champlain: The Birth of French America*, 11–16.

[25] David Hackett Fischer offers a comprehensive summary of the debates regarding Champlain's birth date in *Champlain's Dream*, 569–73.

[26] Ibid., 25; Thierry, "Introduction," in Samuel de Champlain, *Les foundations*, 14–15.

[27] For the evolution of Champlain's religious views, see Dominique Deslandres, "Samuel de Champlain and Religion," in Litalien and Vaugeois, *Champlain: The Birth of French America*, 191–204.

[28] Hackett Fischer, *Champlain's Dream*, 56–57.

[29] Le Blant and Baudry, *Nouveaux documents*, 18.

[30] Samuel de Champlain, *Brief Narrative*, in Biggar et al., *Works*, vol. 1, 3; Buisseret, "The Cartographic Technique of Samuel de Champlain," 257; Hackett Fischer, *Champlain's Dream*, 62–63; Heidenreich and Ritch, *Samuel de Champlain Before 1604*, 24–29.

[31] Samuel de Champlain, *Brief Narrative*, in Biggar et al., *Works*, vol. 1, 3–4.

[32] Samuel de Champlain, *Brief Narrative*, in Biggar et al., *Works*, vol. 1, 4–10; Hackett Fischer, *Champlain's Dream*, 77–82; Heidenreich and Ritch, *Samuel de Champlain Before 1604*, 32–36.

[33] Reproduced in Samuel de Champlain, *Brief Narrative*, in Biggar et al., *Works*, vol. 1, 1–80.

[34] For the history of the manuscript and the controversies surrounding the *Brief Narrative* (*Brief Discours* in French), see François-Marc Gagnon, "Is the *Brief Discours* by Champlain?" in Litalien and Vaugeois, *Champlain: The Birth of French America*, 83–92; Laura Giraudo, "The Manuscripts of the *Brief Discours*," in Litalien and Vaugeois, *Champlain: The Birth of French America*, 63–82; Laura Giraudo, "Research Report: A Mission to Spain," in Litalien and Vaugeois, *Champlain: The Birth of French America*, 93–97; Marcel Trudel, "Samuel de Champlain," in *Dictionary of Canadian Biography*, 187–88.

[35] Samuel de Champlain, *The Voyages* (1632), part 1, in Biggar et al., *Works*, vol. 3, 314–15; Marcel Trudel, *Les vaines tentatives 1524–1603*, vol. 1, *Histoire de la Nouvelle-France*, 252–54.

[36] Marcel Trudel, "Gravé du Pont," in *Dictionary of Canadian Biography*, vol. 1, 345–46.

[37] Heidenreich and Ritch, *Samuel de Champlain Before 1604*, 60–65.

[38] Alain Beaulieu, "The Birth of the Franco-American Alliance," in Litalien and Vaugeois, *Champlain: The Birth of French America*, 153–63; D'Avignon, *Champlain et les fondateurs oubliés*, 475–78; Camille Girard and Édith Gagné, "Première alliance interculturelle: rencontre entre Montagnais et Français à Tadoussac en 1603," *Recherches Amérindiennes au Québec* 25, no. 3 (1995): 3–14; Trudel, *Les vaines tentatives 1524–1603*, 259–61.

[39] For the life of Dugua de Mons, the "forgotten" founder of New France and Champlain's partner and supporter in colonization for two decades, see Guy Binot, *Pierre Dugua de Mons, gentilhomme Royannais, premier colonisateur du Canada, lieutenant général de la Nouvelle-France de 1603 à 1612* (Royan, France: Éditions Bonne Anse, 2004). See also George MacBeath, "Du Gua de Mons, Pierre," in *Dictionary of Canadian Biography*, vol. 1, "De Mons, Pierre Du Gua," 291–94.

[40] Jean-Yves Grenon, "Pierre Dugua de Mons, Lieutenant General of New France," in Litalien and Vaugeois, *Champlain: The Birth of French America*, 143–61; Trudel, *Le Comptoir*, 9–15.

[41] Henry Percival Biggar, *The Early Trading Companies of New France: A Contribution to the History of Commerce and Discovery in North America* (Toronto: University of Toronto Press, 1901), 51–56; Trudel, *Le Comptoir*, 65–68, 91–93.

[42] Huia Ryder, "Biencourt de Poutrincourt et de Saint-Just, Jean de," in *Dictionary of Canadian Biography*, vol. 1, 96–99.

[43] Biggar, *Early Trading Companies*, 18–37; Laurier Turgeon, "The French in New England before Champlain," in Litalien and Vaugeois, *Champlain: The Birth of French America*, 98–112.

[44] This period is covered in Champlain's second work, *The Voyages of the Sieur de Champlain of Saintonge, Captain in the Ordinary for the King in the Navy* (1613), vol. 1, in Biggar et al., *Works*, as well as in Lescarbot, *History of New France*, vol. 2. See also Hackett Fischer, *Champlain's Dream*, 174–223.

[45] Hackett Fischer, *Champlain's Dream*, 214–17; Éric Thierry, "A Creation of Champlain's: The Order of Good Cheer," in Litalien and Vaugeois, *Champlain: The Birth of French America*, 135–49.

[46] The best history of New France during this period of Champlain's career is Trudel's *Histoire de la Nouvelle-France*, vol. 2. Much of the information in this and the following paragraphs can be found discussed in more detail in that volume. Champlain recounts the history of this period in Book Two of his *The Voyages of the Sieur de Champlain of Saintonge, Captain in the Ordinary for the King in the Navy* (1613), reproduced in Biggar et al., *Works*, vol. 2. See also Hackett Fischer, *Champlain's Dream*, 227–36.

[47] Albert Tessier, "Boullé, Eustache," in *Dictionary of Canadian Biography*, vol. 1, 109–10; Marie-Emmanuel Chabot, "Boullé, Hélène," in *Dictionary of Canadian Biography*, vol. 1, 110.

[48] Hackett Fischer, *Champlain's Dream*, note 48, 687.

[49] Samuel de Champlain, *The Voyages* (1613), in Biggar et al., *Works*, vol. 2, 119, and Samuel de Champlain, *Voyages and Discoveries* (1619), in Biggar et al., *Works*, vol. 3, 31; Gaétan Gervais, "Champlain and Ontario (1603–35)," in Litalien and Vaugeois, *Champlain: The Birth of French America*, 180–90; Hackett Fischer, *Champlain's Dream*, 317–27; Trudel, *Histoire de la Nouvelle France*, vol. 2, 195–98, 215–19.

[50] The volume bears the copyright date of 1613 but, as Éric Thierry points out, was not actually printed until early 1614, precisely so that Champlain could include an account of his exploits in the summer of 1613. See Thierry's "Introduction," in *À la rencontre des Algonquins et des Hurons 1612–1619*, ed. Éric Thierry (Québec: Les Éditions du Septentrion, 2009), 7, 26.

[51] Samuel de Champlain, *The Voyages* (1632), part 2, in Biggar et al., *Works*, vol. 5, 71–80, 124.

[52] Published, along with the response of the Chamber of Commerce, in Biggar et al., *Works*, vol. 2, 326–51.

[53] "Contract between Louis Hébert and the Company of Canada" (March 6, 1617), in Le Blant and Baudry, *Nouveaux documents*, no. 160, 361–62.

[54] Samuel de Champlain, *Voyages and Discoveries* (1619), in Biggar et al., *Works*, vol. 3, 177–202.

[55] Samuel de Champlain, *The Voyages* (1632), in Biggar et al., *Works*, vol. 5, 1–2.

[56] Paul-Louis Martin, "Domestication of the Countryside and Provision of Supplies," in Litalien and Vaugeois, *Champlain: The Birth of New France*, 205–10; see also John A. Dickinson, "Champlain, Administrator," in Litalien and Vaugeois, *Champlain: The Birth of New France*, 211–17.

[57] Samuel de Champlain, *The Voyages* (1613), in Biggar et al., *Works*, vol. 2, 25–32.

PART TWO

The Documents

1

Explorer

1

SAMUEL DE CHAMPLAIN

On Exploring the Coast of Norumbega [Maine]

1604

Between 1604 and 1606 Champlain participated in three voyages of exploration in the region of Acadia known in the seventeenth century as Norumbega (most likely from a Wabanaki word), today's Maine. During these voyages the French carefully surveyed the Atlantic shoreline from Maine to Cape Cod, Massachusetts. Champlain commanded the first of these voyages, which concentrated on the coast of Maine and included as well an expedition up the Penobscot River. Pierre Dugua, Sieur de Mons (born ca. 1581), commanded the subsequent voyage to the region, and Jean de Biencourt, Sieur de Poutrincourt (1557–1615), the third and final one.

For the first expedition, described in this excerpt from Champlain's The Voyages of the Sieur de Champlain of Saintonge, Captain in the Ordinary for the King in the Navy *(1613), Champlain sailed in a small vessel called a* patache *designed specifically for exploring coasts and brought along as well both a birch bark canoe and a small skiff, which permitted him to sail up rivers that were too shallow for the patache. Champlain had with him on this voyage two Natives from the Etchemin nation, who inhabited the territory north and east of the*

Samuel de Champlain, *The Voyages of the Sieur de Champlain of Saintonge, Captain in the Ordinary for the King in the Navy* (1613), vol. 1, bk. 1, trans. W. F. Ganong, in *The Works of Samuel de Champlain*, ed. Henry Percival Biggar et al. (Toronto: Champlain Society, 1922–1935; Toronto: University of Toronto Press, 1971), 280–98.

Penobscot River and thus were familiar with the territory Champlain was exploring. Although not insensitive to the beauty of a scenic wilderness, Champlain's utilitarian focus on finding places that could be cultivated and thus become the home of a French colony led him to prefer fields over forests and flat potential farmland over mountains, a preference reflected in this document.

After the departure of the vessels, the Sieur de Monts decided, in order not to lose time, to send and explore along the coast of Norumbega, and entrusted to me this duty, which I found very agreeable.

For this purpose I set out from Ste. Croix on September 2 in a small vessel of seventeen to eighteen tons, with twelve sailors and two Indians to serve us as guides to the places with which they were acquainted. That day we met with the vessels having on board the Sieur de Poutrincourt, which lay at anchor at the mouth of the river Ste. Croix on account of the bad weather. From this place we could not set out until the fifth of the said month, and when we were two or three leagues at sea the fog came up so thick that we immediately lost sight of their vessels. Continuing our course along the coast we made this day some twenty-five leagues, and passed a great number of islands, sand-banks, shoals, and rocks, which in some places project more than four leagues out to sea. We named these islands the Ordered Islands. The greater part of them are covered with pines, firs, and other inferior woods. Among these islands are many ports which are attractive and safe, but unsuitable for settlement. That same day we also passed near an island about four or five leagues in length, off which we were almost lost on a little rock, level with the surface of the water, which made a hole in our pinnace close to the keel. The distance from this island to the mainland on the north is not a hundred paces. It is very high and cleft in places, giving it the appearance from the sea of seven or eight mountains one alongside the other. The tops of most of them are bare of trees, because there is nothing there but rocks. The woods consist only of pines, firs, and birches. I named it Mount Desert island. Its latitude is 44° 30′.

The next day, the sixth of the month, we made two leagues, and caught sight of smoke in a cove which was at the foot of the mountains above-mentioned; and we saw two canoes paddled by Indians, who came to observe us at a distance of a musket-shot. I sent our two Indians in a canoe to assure them of our friendship, but the fear they had of us made them turn back. The next morning they returned, and came alongside our pinnace, and held converse with our Indians. I had some biscuit, tobacco, and sundry other trifles given to them. These Indians had come to hunt beaver, and to catch fish, some of which they gave us. Having made friends with them, they guided us into their river Peimtegouet [lower Penobscot below Bangor], as they call it, where they told us lived their chief named Bessabez, headman of that river. I believe that this river is the one which several pilots and historians call Norumbega, and which most of them have described as large and spacious, with a number of islands, and with its entrance in latitude 43°, or 43° 30', though others give 44°, more or less. As to the magnetic variation, I have never read nor heard any mention of it. They also described how there is a great town thickly peopled with skilled and clever Indians who use cotton thread. I am convinced that the majority of those who mention it never saw it, and speak of it only by hearsay from people who had no more knowledge of it than themselves. I can well believe that some may have seen its mouth, because in fact there are numerous islands there, and the latitude thereof is 44°, as they state; but there is no evidence whatever that any one ever entered it; for they would have described it differently in order to remove the doubts of many people on this score. . . .

Now to return to the continuation of our journey. Entering the river one sees fine islands, which are very pleasant on account of their beautiful meadows. We went as far as a place to which the Indians guided us, where the river is not over an eighth of a league in width; and here, some two hundred paces from the west shore and level with the surface of the water, is a rock which is dangerous. Thence to isle Haute it is fifteen leagues. After making some seven or eight leagues from this narrows (which is the narrowest spot we found), we came to a little river [Kenduskeag] in the vicinity of which we had to anchor, for the reason that before us we saw a great many rocks which are exposed at low tide, and moreover, had we wished to go on, we could not have proceeded more than half a league on account of a waterfall which descends a slope of some seven to eight feet. This I saw when I went there in a canoe with the Indians we had with us, where we found only enough water for a canoe. But below the fall, which is some two hundred paces in width, the river is beautiful; and is unobstructed as far as the place where we had anchored. I landed to see the country; and going hunting, found the part I visited most pleasant and agreeable. One would think the oaks there had been planted designedly. I saw few firs, but on one side of the river were some pines, while on the other were all oaks, together with underwood which extends far inland. And I shall add that from the mouth of the river to the spot where we were, a distance of some twenty-five leagues, we saw neither town nor village, nor any traces that there ever had been any, but only one or two empty Indian wigwams which were constructed in the same manner as those of the Souriquois, that is, covered with tree-bark. So far as we could judge there are few Indians on this river, and these also are called Etechemins. They come there and to the islands only for a few months in summer during the fishing and hunting season, when game is plentiful. They are a people with no fixed abode, from what I have discovered and learned from themselves; for they pass the winter sometimes in one place and sometimes in another, wheresoever they perceive the hunting of wild animals is the best. Upon these they live when hunger presses, without putting anything aside for their support during the famines, which sometimes are severe.

Now this river must of necessity be that of Norumbega; for, after it, there is no other in the above-mentioned latitudes as far as 41°, to which we went, except the Kennebec, which is nearly in the same latitude, but of no great size. Moreover, there can be none here which extend far inland, because the great river St. Lawrence runs parallel to the coast of Acadia and of Norumbega, and the distance between them by land is not above forty-five leagues, or sixty at the widest part, as may be seen on my map.

I shall now leave this subject in order to return to the Indians, who had conducted me to the falls of Norumbega river, and who had gone to inform Bessabez their chief, and other Indians. They [in their turn] went to another little river to inform also their chief, whose name was Cabahis, and to notify him of our arrival.

On the sixteenth of the month, some thirty Indians came to us upon the assurance given to them by those who had acted as our guides. On the same day the above-mentioned Bessabez also came to see us with six canoes. As soon as the Indians on shore saw him arrive, they all began to sing, dance, and leap, until he had landed, after which they all seated themselves on the ground in a circle, according to their custom when they wish to make a speech or hold a festival. Cabahis, the other chief, also arrived a little later, with twenty or thirty of his companions, who kept by themselves; and they were much pleased to see us, inasmuch as it was the first time they had ever beheld Christians. Some time afterwards I landed with two of my companions and two of our Indians who acted as our interpreters. I ordered the crew of our pinnace to draw near the Indians, and to hold their weapons in readiness to do their duty in case they perceived any movement of these people against us. Bessabez, seeing us on shore, bade us sit down, and began with his companions to smoke, as they usually do before beginning their speeches. They made us a present of venison and waterfowl.

I directed our interpreter to tell our Indians that they were to make Bessabez, Cabahis, and their companions understand that the Sieur de Monts had sent me to them to see them, and also their country; that he wished to remain friends with them, and reconcile them with their enemies, the Souriquois and Canadians; moreover, that he desired to settle in their country and show them how to cultivate it, in order that they might no longer lead so miserable an existence as they were doing; and several other remarks on the same subject. This our Indians made them understand, whereat they signified that they were well satisfied, declaring that no greater benefit could come to them than to have our friendship; and that they desired us to settle in their country, and wished to live in peace with their enemies, in order that in future they might hunt the beaver more than they had ever done, and barter these beaver with us in exchange for things necessary for their usage. When he had finished his speech, I made them presents of hatchets, rosaries, caps, knives, and other little knick-knacks; then we separated. The rest of this day and the following night they did nothing but dance, sing, and make merry, awaiting the dawn, when we bartered a certain number of beaver-skins. Afterwards each returned, Bessabez with his companions in their direction and we in ours, well pleased to make acquaintance with these people.

On the seventeenth of the month I made an observation, and found the latitude to be 45° 25'. This done, we set out for another river called Kennebec, distant from this place thirty-five leagues, and from Bedabedec about twenty. The tribe of Indians at Kennebec is called Etechemins, like those of Norumbega.

On the eighteenth of the month we passed near a little river where lived Cabahis, who accompanied us in our pinnace some twelve leagues. Having asked him about the source of Norumbega river, he informed me that after passing the fall of which I have made mention above, and travelling some distance up the river, one entered a lake through which they go to the river of Ste. Croix, thence they go a short distance overland, and then enter the river of the Etechemins. Furthermore, into this lake falls another river, up which they travel several days, and afterwards enter another lake and pass through the midst of it; then, having reached the end of it, they travel again some distance overland and afterwards enter another little river that empties a league from Quebec, which is on the great river St. Lawrence. All these peoples of Norumbega are very swarthy, and are clothed in beaver-skins and other furs like the Canadian Indians and the Souriquois; and they have the same manner of life.

2

SAMUEL DE CHAMPLAIN

On Attempts to Visit the "Inland Sea"
(Hudson's Bay)
1613

In 1613 Champlain sailed to New France, taking with him a young man named Nicolas de Vignau, who years earlier Champlain had sent to live among the Ottawa to learn their language. Vignau, while in France in 1613, told Champlain that the Ottawa had taken Vignau to an inland sea, probably Hudson's Bay, where he had seen the remnants of an English shipwreck, and heard of a white boy captive whom the Natives of the region wished to hand over to Champlain. Champlain had read the recently published account of Henry Hudson's disastrous 1610–1611 voyage, during which Hudson's men had mutinied and set him, his young son, and the remaining loyal sailors adrift on Hudson's Bay. He was also well aware of the strong interest of the French government, as well as that of the English, in discovering a Northwest Passage to Asia. Although Champlain was suspicious of Vignau's tale, Vignau repeatedly vowed he was telling the truth, and since Vignau's story coincided with Champlain's own ambition to find a Northwest Passage, Champlain brought Vignau along on the 1613 voyage. The official publication date of this volume is 1613, although in fact it was not printed until early in 1614 after Champlain had returned from his voyage of summer 1613 and added to the manuscript the section recounting his exploits of 1613, including the material in this excerpt.

Having then but two canoes, I was able to take with me only four men, among whom was one named Nicolas de Vignau, the most impudent liar that has been seen for a long time, as the continuation of this story will show. He had some time before this wintered with the Indians and I had sent him on explorations in previous years. On returning to Paris

Samuel de Champlain, *Fourth Voyage of the Sieur de Champlain Captain in Ordinary to the King in the Navy* (1613), vol. 2, trans. W. F. Ganong, in *The Works of Samuel de Champlain*, ed. Henry Percival Biggar et al. (Toronto: Champlain Society, 1922–1935; Toronto: University of Toronto Press, 1971), 255–96.

in the year 1612 he had reported to me that he had seen the northern sea [Hudson's Bay]; that the river of the Algonquins [the Ottawa] came from a lake which emptied into it; and that in seventeen days one could go from the St. Louis rapids to this sea and back again. He said also that he had seen pieces of the wreck of an English ship which had been lost on that coast, on which were eighty men who had escaped to land. These the Indians killed because these Englishmen tried to take from them by force their Indian corn and other supplies. He said too that he had seen the scalps of these men which these Indians according to their custom had cut off. These they would show me, and would also give me an English boy whom they were keeping for me. This intelligence had pleased me greatly; for I thought I had found close at hand what I was searching for a long way off. Thus I besought him to tell me the truth, so that I might inform the king, and warned him that if he were telling a lie, he was putting a rope about his neck, but that if his story were true, he could count upon being well rewarded. He again asserted the truth of it with greater oaths than ever. And in order the better to play his part he presented me with an account of the country which he said he had drawn up to the best of his ability. His self-assurance, the honesty of which I judged him to be possessed, the account he had drawn up, the broken fragments of the ship and the points already mentioned, had great show of truth, coupled with the voyage of the English towards Labrador in 1612, where they found a strait into which they sailed as far as the sixty-third degree of latitude and the two hundred and ninetieth of longitude. They spent the winter near the fifty-third degree and lost some ships as their account shows. These things leading me to believe his story, I thereupon made a report of it to the Chancellor [Nicolas Brûlart de Sillery], which I also showed to the Maréchal de Brissac and to Chief Justice Jeannin as well as to other Lords of the Court who told me that I ought to see the thing for myself. For this reason I asked the Sieur Georges, a La Rochelle merchant, to give Vignau a passage in his ship, which he willingly did. On board the ship, Georges questioned him as to why he was making the trip, and since it was of no profit to him, he asked him whether he expected any wages. De Vignau answered that he did not, nor did he look for anything from anyone but the king, and that he was undertaking the journey solely for the purpose of show- ing me the northern sea which he had visited. And at La Rochelle he made a solemn declaration in the matter to the Sieur Georges before two notaries.

Now when on Whitsunday I was taking leave of everybody and par- ticularly of all the chief men to whose prayers I commended myself, I said to Vignau in their presence that if what he had previously stated was not true, he should spare me the trouble of undertaking this journey, which would inevitably involve many risks. He reasserted, on peril of his life, all he had previously stated.

Accordingly, our canoes being laden with provisions, with our arms, and with goods with which to make presents to the Indians, I set out on Monday, May 27, from St. Helen's island [near Montréal] with four Frenchmen and an Indian, a farewell salute being given me with a few rounds from small pieces. That day we went only as far as the St. Louis rapids which is but a league farther up, on account of the bad weather which prevented us from going any farther.

On the twenty-ninth we passed the rapid partly by portage, partly by tracking,[1] and were forced to carry our canoes, clothes, provisions, and arms on our shoulders, which is no small labour for those who are not used to it. Having left it two leagues behind, we entered a lake [Lake St. Louis] some twelve leagues in circumference into which empty three rivers, one coming from the west [St. Lawrence River], from the direction of the Ochataiguins [Tribe of the Huron confederacy], who are distant one hundred and fifty or two hundred leagues from the Great Rapids; another from the south [Chateauguay], which is the country of the Iroquois, a like distance away; and the third from the North [the Ottawa River], where the Algonquins and the Nebicerini live, about the same distance away. This northern river, according to the report of the Indians, comes from a greater distance and some three hundred leagues away passes through tribes unknown to them. . . .

On Saturday, June 1, we passed two more rapids, the first being half a league long, and the second a league. Here we had much labour; for so great is the swiftness of the current that it makes a dreadful noise, and, falling from level to level, produces everywhere such a white foam that no water at all is seen. This rapid is strewn with rocks and in it here and there are some islands covered with pines and white cedars. It was here we had such difficulty, for being unable to portage our canoes on account of the thickness of the woods, we had to track them, and in pulling mine I nearly lost my life, because the canoe turned broadside into a whirlpool, and had I not luckily fallen between two rocks, the canoe would have dragged me in, since I could not quickly enough loosen the rope which was twisted round my hand, which hurt me very much, and nearly cut it off. In this danger I cried aloud to God and began to pull my canoe towards me, which was sent back to me by an eddy such as

---

[1] By pulling them through the water, since they were moving upstream and thus could not simply "shoot" the rapids.

occurs in these rapids. Having escaped, I gave praise to God, beseeching Him to preserve us. . . .

On the following day in a river, after we had passed a small lake four leagues long and two wide, we met with fifteen canoes of Indians called Quenongebin [the Algonquin Kinounchepirini], who had been informed of my coming by the Indians who had passed by the St. Louis rapids on their return from warring with the Iroquois. I was very glad to meet them, and they me, and they were astonished to see me in that country with so few Frenchmen, and with only one Indian. Hence, having saluted each other after the manner of the country, I requested them not to pass on until I had declared my wishes to them. To this they agreed and we went and camped on an island.

The next day I explained to them that I had gone into their country to see them and to keep the promise I had previously made to them. I told them that if they were resolved to go to war, I should be much pleased, since I had brought men for that purpose, at which they expressed much satisfaction; but when I informed them that I wished to go on farther to warn the other tribes, they tried to dissuade me, declaring that the way was bad and that we had hitherto seen nothing like it. On this account, I begged them to give me one of their men to steer our second canoe, and also to act as guide; for our guides were no longer acquainted with the country. They did so readily, and as a reward I made them a present, and lent them one of our Frenchmen whom we least needed. Him I sent back to the Rapids, with a leaf out of a note-book, whereon, for lack of paper, I sent them news of what I was doing.

Thus we separated; and continuing our journey up the said river, we came upon another, very beautiful and wide, which flows from a nation called Ouescharini [an Algonquin people], who live to the north of it and four days' journey from its mouth. This river is very attractive, on account of the beautiful islands in it, and of the lands along its banks covered with fine open woods. This land is suitable for tillage. . . .

On the sixth we left this island of Ste. Croix, where the river is a league and a half wide, and having gone eight or ten leagues we passed a small rapid by paddling and also a number of islands of different sizes.[2] Here our Indians left their sacks with their provisions and their less

---

[2] Vignau and Champlain's Native guides began to compete here for Champlain's loyalty, as Vignau wanted to take a different route to their destination, Allumette Lake, than did Champlain's Native guides. Champlain states that Vignau, fearful that his lie would be uncovered, hoped that if he could persuade Champlain to take a longer, more difficult, route Champlain would be killed or become discouraged, thus avoiding the moment of reckoning when Vignau's dishonesty would be revealed. Of course, we only have Champlain's word here, and we do not know what Vignau's real motives were.

necessary articles, in order to be lighter for portaging, and avoiding several rapids which had to be passed. There was a great dispute between our Indians and our impostor, who declared that there was no danger by the rapids and that we should go that way. Our Indians said to him, "You are tired of living," and to me that I should not believe him and that he was not speaking the truth. Having observed several times in this way that he had no knowledge of these places, I followed the advice of the Indians; and it was lucky I did so; for he was on the look-out for difficult places in which to work my destruction, or to disgust me with the undertaking, as he afterwards confessed, whereof mention will be made farther on. We crossed to the west of the river, which flowed towards the north, and took the latitude of this place, which was 46° 40′. We had much trouble in taking this route overland, being laden for my part alone with three arquebuses, an equal number of paddles, my cloak, and some small articles. I encouraged our men, who were somewhat more heavily laden, but who suffered more from mosquitoes than from their loads. Thus, after passing four small ponds and walking two leagues and a half, we were so tired that it was impossible for us to go farther; for it was nearly twenty-four hours since we had eaten anything but a little broiled fish, without any other dish; for we had left our provisions behind as I have stated above. Therefore, we rested on the bank of a pond which was quite pleasant; and we made a smudge[3] to drive away the mosquitoes which annoyed us greatly. Their pertinacity is so great that it is impossible to give any description of it. We set our nets to catch some fish. . . .

[The following day] . . . we reached a lake, six leagues long and two wide, so abundant in fish that the surrounding tribes do their fishing here. Near this lake is a settlement of Indians who till the land and reap the maize. Their chief, whose name is Nibachis, came with his men to see us, and was astonished that we had been able to pass the rapids and bad trails on the way to their country. And having, according to their custom, offered us tobacco, he began to address his companions, saying that we must have fallen from the clouds; for he did not know how we had been able to get through, when those who live in the country had great difficulty in coming along such difficult trails, giving them to understand that I carried out all I set my mind upon.

* * *

---

[3] Ointment smeared on the body like sunscreen, usually made with a base of animal fat, that the Natives used to repel mosquitoes.

Nibachis had two canoes fitted out to take me to see another chief named Tessoüat, who lived eight leagues from him on the shore of a large lake, through which passes the river we had left, which leads northward. Thus we crossed the lake [Muskrat Lake] in a west-north-westerly direction nearly seven leagues, where having landed we went a league to the north-east, through a very beautiful region along narrow beaten trails where the going is easy, and we arrived at the shore of this lake where stood Tessoüat's encampment [on Lower Allumette Lake]. He was with another neighbouring chief, and was much astonished at seeing me, telling us he thought I was a ghost, and that he could not believe his eyes. Thence we went over to an island [Morrison or Hawley Island] where stood their badly-made bark wigwams. This island is covered with oaks, pines, and elms, and is not liable to be flooded as are the other islands in the lake.

This island is strongly situated; for at its two ends and where the river enters the lake are troublesome rapids, whose rugged character makes it strong. The Indians have made their encampment here in order to escape the incursions of their enemies. The island is in latitude 47°, as is also the lake, which is twenty leagues long and three or four wide. It abounds in fish, but the hunting is not very good.

Now, as I looked about the island, I noticed their cemeteries, and was filled with wonder at the sight of the tombs, in the form of shrines, made of pieces of wood, crossed at the top, and fixed upright in the ground three feet apart or thereabouts. Above the cross-pieces they place a large piece of wood, and in front another standing upright, on which is carved rudely (as one might expect) the face of him or her who is there buried. If it is a man they put up a shield, a sword with a handle such as they use, a club, a bow and arrows; if it is a chief, he will have a bunch of feathers on his head and some other ornament or embellishment; if a child, they give him a bow and arrow; if a woman or girl, a kettle, an earthen pot, a wooden spoon, and a paddle. The largest tomb is six or seven feet long and four wide; the others smaller. They are painted yellow and red, with various decorations as fine as the carving. The dead man is buried in his beaver or other skin, whereof he made use in his life; and they place beside him all his valuables such as axes, knives, kettles and awls, so that these things may be of use to him in the land whither he goes; for they believe in the immortality of the soul as I have stated elsewhere. These carved tombs are only made for warriors; for other men they put no more on the tombs than for women, as being useless people. Hence but few of these tombs are found amongst them. . . .

On the following day all the guests came, each with his wooden bowl and spoon, and sat down on the ground in Tessoüat's wigwam without observing any rank or ceremony. . . .

When the banquet was over, the young men, who are not present at the speeches and council-meetings, and who during banquets remain at the doors of the wigwams, left. Then each of those who had stayed began to fill his pipe, and several offered me theirs, and we spent a full half-hour at this ceremony, without uttering a word, as is their custom.

After having smoked plentifully during such a long silence, I explained to them through my interpreter, that the object of my journey was none other than to assure them of my affection, and of my desire to aid them in their wars, as I had done previously: that what had hindered me from coming last year as I had promised, was that the king had employed me in other wars, but that he had now commanded me to visit them, and to reassure them regarding these things, and that for this purpose I had a number of men at the St. Louis rapids. I told them I had come on a visit to their country to note the fertility of the soil, the lakes, rivers and sea, which they had told me were in their country, and that I desired to visit a nation, distant six days' march from them, called the Nebicerini, in order to invite them also to go on the war-path, and that for this purpose I asked them to give me four canoes, with eight Indians to take me to that region. And since the Algonquins are not great friends of the Nebicerini, they seemed to listen to me with the greater attention.

My speech being finished, they began again to smoke and to converse together quietly about my proposals. Then Tessoüat, on behalf of all, began to speak, saying that they had always realized that I was more kindly disposed towards them than any other Frenchman they had seen, and that the proofs of it which they had experienced in the past, made it the more easy for them to believe in it for the future; that I had shown that I was indeed their friend by running so many risks to come and visit them, and to invite them to go on the war-path; and that all this forced them to bear as much good will towards me as to their own children. Nevertheless that last year I had failed to keep my promise and that two thousand Indians had come to the Rapids in the hope of finding me, in order to go on the war-path and to make me gifts; that on not finding me they were much disappointed, thinking I was dead, as some had told them; moreover, that the French who were at the Rapids were unwilling to assist them in their wars, and some had even treated them badly, so that they had resolved among themselves not to come to the Rapids any more. This had forced them, since they did not expect to see me again, to go on the war-path alone, and in fact twelve hundred of their men had done so. And since the greater part of their warriors were absent, they requested me to postpone the project until the following year, when they would make it known to all the tribes of that region. As for the four canoes for which I asked, they granted them to me, but with much hesitation, declaring that they viewed such an enterprise with considerable disfavour, on account of the toils I should undergo; that these tribes were sorcerers and had killed many of Tessoüat's people by magic and poisoning, and consequently were not considered friendly; moreover as regards war, I had no need of them, for they had small courage. With this and various other arguments they tried to dissuade me from my project.

I, on the other hand, whose one desire was to see these tribes, and to make friends with them, in order to view the northern sea, made light of their difficulties, saying that it was not far to [Nebicerini] country; that as for the bad portages, these could not be worse than those we had already passed, and that with respect to their spells, these would have no power to hurt me; for my God would preserve me from them; that I was also acquainted with their herbs, and should therefore take good care not to eat them; that I wished to make them all good friends and would make presents to the other tribes for that purpose, feeling sure that they would do something for me. In response to these reasons they granted me the four canoes, as I have stated, whereat I was much pleased, and forgot all my past troubles in the hope of seeing that much-desired sea.

To while away the rest of the day I went for a walk in their gardens, which had in them only some pumpkins, beans, and peas like ours, which they are beginning to grow. Here Thomas my interpreter, who understands their language very well, came to tell me that the Indians, after I had left them, had imagined that if I should undertake this journey, I should die, and they as well, and that they could not give me the canoes as they had promised, inasmuch as no one among them was willing to be my guide. But they thought that I should postpone the journey till the following year, when they would take me along with them, with a good escort to protect ourselves against these tribes, who are wicked people, in case they wished to do us harm.

This news grieved me greatly, and at once I went off to find them, and told them that till then I had held them to be men and true to their word; but that now they were showing themselves children and liars, and that if they did not wish to keep their promises, they should not pretend to be my friends; however, if they felt inconvenienced by giving me four canoes, they could give me but two, and only four Indians.

They again represented to me the difficulties of the portages, the number of rapids, the wickedness of those tribes, and that it was on account of the fear they entertained of my destruction that they were refusing my request.

I replied to them that I was sorry they showed themselves so little my friends, and that I should never have believed it; that I had a youth (pointing to my impostor) who had been in that country and had not noticed all the difficulties they represented, nor found those tribes as bad as they were saying. They then began to eye him, and particularly Tessoüat, the old chief, with whom he had wintered, who calling him by name, said to him in his language, "Nicholas, is it true that you have said you had been in the Nebicerini country?" For a long time he remained silent; then he said to them in their language which he speaks a little, "Yes, I have been there." Immediately they regarded him with anger, and rushed upon him, as if they would have eaten him or torn him asunder, shouting very loudly. And Tessoüat said to him, "You are a brazen liar; you know well that every night you slept alongside of me and my children, and rose every morning at that place. If you visited those tribes, it was in your sleep. Why have you been so shamefaced as to tell lies to your chief, and so wicked as to wish to jeopardize his life amid so many dangers? You are a miserable wretch whom he ought to put to death more cruelly than we do our enemies. I am not surprised that he importuned us so much, having confidence in what you told him." I at once said to him that he would have to make a reply to these people, and that since he had been in those parts, he must give evidence of this to convince me, and to get me out of the difficulty in which he had placed me; but he remained silent and quite abashed.

I immediately drew him aside from the Indians, and begged him earnestly to tell me the truth; and said that if he had seen this sea, I would have the promised reward given to him, and that if he had not seen it, he must tell me so, without giving me any more worry. Once more with oaths he affirmed all that he had before asserted, and said he would show me this if these Indians would give us the canoes.

After this talk Thomas came and told me that the Indians of the island were secretly sending a canoe to the Nebicerini to warn them of my arrival. Thereupon, in order to profit by this opportunity, I went to these Indians to tell them that that night I had dreamed that they were going to send a canoe to the Nebicerini without letting me know, at which I was astonished, seeing that they knew that I wished to go there. To this they replied that I did them great wrong, in that I had more confidence in a liar, who wanted to kill me, than in so many honest chiefs, who were my friends, and held my life dear. I answered them that my man (speaking of our impostor) had been in that region with one of Tessoüat's relations and had seen the sea, and the broken fragments of an English ship, together with eighty scalps in the possession of the Indians, and an English youth whom they kept prisoner and these they wished to present to me.

On hearing this mention of the sea, the ships, the English scalps and the prisoner, they exclaimed more loudly than before that he was a liar, and such they have since called him as the greatest insult they could offer to him. With one voice they declared that he should be put to death, or that he should name the person with whom he had gone there, and should state the lakes, rivers and trails by which he had passed. To this he replied without flinching that he had forgotten the name of this Indian, although he had mentioned his name to me more than twenty times, and even on the previous day. As for the particulars of the country, he had described them in a paper which he had given to me. Then I showed his map and had it interpreted to the Indians who questioned him regarding it. To this he made no reply, but by his sullen silence manifested his wickedness.

My mind being in doubt, I withdrew by myself and went over the particulars of the expedition of the English, already given, and found our impostor's statements to be quite in harmony with these. Moreover there was little likelihood of this youth having invented all this and of his not having made the journey. It was more likely that he had seen these things but that his ignorance did not allow him to reply to the questions of the Indians. Furthermore, if the account of the English is true, this northern sea cannot be farther off than one hundred leagues of latitude; for I was in latitude 47°, and in longitude 296°, but it may be that the difficulty of passing the rapids, and the ruggedness of the mountains covered with snow, have prevented these tribes from having knowledge of this sea. Indeed, they have always told me that it is only thirty-five or forty days' journey from the country of the Ochataiguins to the ocean, which is in sight at three places. This they assured me again this year, but no one had spoken to me of this northern sea, save this impostor, who had greatly cheered me on account of the short distance to it.

Now while this canoe was being got ready, I sent for him to come before his companions; and informing him of all that had taken place, I told him that the time for dissimulation was past, and that he must tell me whether or not he had seen the things he had related; I said that I wished to seize the opportunity that presented itself; that I had forgotten all that had happened, but that if I had to proceed farther, I should have him hanged and strangled without any mercy. After some meditation he fell upon his knees and asked me for pardon, declaring that all he had stated regarding this sea both in France and in this country was false; that he had never seen it, and had never been farther than Tessoüat's village; and that he had related these things in order to return to Canada. In a transport of rage at this I had him removed, being no longer able to endure his presence, and I gave Thomas orders to inquire carefully into the whole affair. To Thomas he persisted in saying that he had had no idea I would undertake this expedition, on account of its dangers, hoping some difficulty might arise, which would prevent me from going farther, such as this with these Indians, who had refused to give me canoes. In this way he hoped the journey would be put off for another year, while he on reaching France would secure a reward for his discovery. Moreover that if I would leave him in this country he would go on until he had found this sea, even should he die in the attempt. These are his words as reported to me by Thomas, and they did not give me much satisfaction; for I was astonished at the effrontery and wickedness of this liar. And I cannot imagine how he invented this falsehood, except that he had heard of the expedition of the English, mentioned above, and in the hope of having some reward, as he said, had been bold enough to put forward this story.

Shortly afterwards and very sorrowfully I went and informed the Indians of the deceit of this liar, telling them that he had confessed the truth to me. At this they were much pleased, but reproached me with having had so little confidence in them, who were chiefs, my friends, and men who always spoke the truth. "This very wicked liar must die," said they; "do you not see that he wanted to kill you? Give him to us, and we promise you he will tell no more lies." And because they were all howling to get at him, and their children still more loudly, I forbade them to do him any harm, and made them also keep their children from doing so, inasmuch as I wished to bring him back to the Rapids to show him to those gentlemen to whom he was to bring salt water; and I said that when I got there, I should consider what was to be done with him.

2

Navigator, Cartographer, and Illustrator

3

GUILLEMME LEVASSEUR

A Map of the Atlantic Ocean

1601

*Champlain's skill as a cartographer and his significant contributions
to European cartographical knowledge about the New World are immediately apparent when his map of 1607 (Document 4) is compared to
this 1601 rendering by another expert French cartographer, Guillemme
Levasseur. Levasseur belonged to the Dieppe School of Cartography, so
named because the Norman port city of Dieppe was home in the late sixteenth century to some of the most accomplished mapmakers in Europe.
The works of the Dieppe mapmakers rivaled the best of maps produced
in the centers of European cartography at the time in Spain and the Low
Countries. Levasseur's map, however, although reflecting some of the most
up-to-date geographical knowledge of the age, is in an older style called
a "mappa mundi" or world map. These often colorful, highly decorative
maps were usually produced for noble or royal patrons for the purpose
of impressing clients or visitors with the command of territory and/or
geographical knowledge that the map's owner possessed. As a result, they
focused more on demarcating the limits of empire than on carefully and
accurately mapping territory in a manner that was of practical use to
explorers or colonial administrators.*

Guillemme Levasseur, *A Map of the Atlantic Ocean* (Dieppe, 1601), Bibliothèque Nationale, Paris.

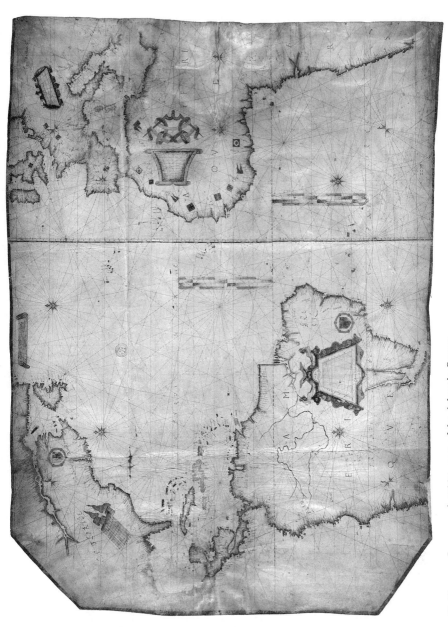

Guillemme Levasseur's 1601 map of the Atlantic Ocean.

4

SAMUEL DE CHAMPLAIN

A Map of the Atlantic Coast from Acadia to Nantucket Sound

1607

In contrast to Levasseur's map, Champlain's map of the same region, produced in 1607, reflects his military training as an ordinance officer. It covers the approximately 1,200 miles of coastline Champlain explored between May 1604 and September 1607. One of the best maps Champlain produced, it represents the earliest accurate (given the limitations of early modern surveying equipment) chart of the Atlantic coast from Acadia (present-day Nova Scotia) to Nantucket Sound (Massachusetts). In it Champlain carefully notes resources that could be of use to the French, such as mines, harbors, and possible river routes to the interior. It displays clearly Champlain's skill as a cartographer and his focus on the practical utility of maps. Still, this map also had propaganda value, showing in particular the territory and resources that would-be French colonizers could hope to appropriate in the New World. But its basic conceptualization of the best way for the French to stake their claims in the New World, by exploring and carefully mapping territory, is also quite different from that of Levasseur's map.

Samuel de Champlain, Samuel de Champlain's map of 1607, plate lxxx, in *The Works of Samuel de Champlain*, ed. Henry Percival Biggar et al. (Toronto: Champlain Society, 1922–1935; Toronto: University of Toronto Press, 1971).

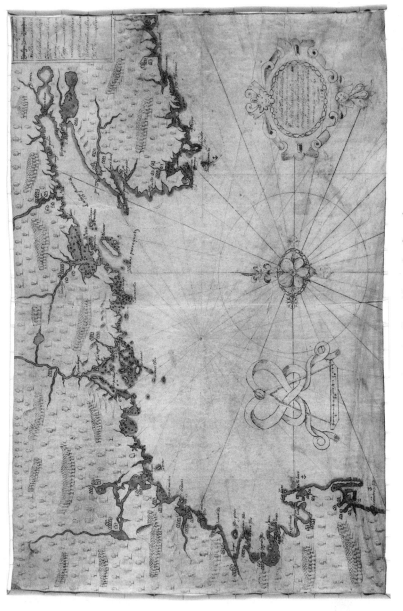

Champlain's 1607 map of the Atlantic coast from Acadia to Nantucket Sound.

5

SAMUEL DE CHAMPLAIN

A Map of New France for the Literate Public

1612

Perhaps Champlain's best map, the map of 1612 is certainly his most beautiful and lavishly illustrated. It incorporates all his discoveries up to the end of 1612, and he intended that it be used as an aid for navigation and to illustrate for the literate public in France the vast territory, resources, and peoples of the New World. This map thus combines the more "showy" mappa mundi tradition in which Levasseur and many other mapmakers in early modern Europe were working with the newer, more utilitarian style using the latest advances in surveying techniques that was gradually developing. While the 1612 map displays Champlain's skills as a cartographer, it is also rich with what map scholars call "iconography," meaning inset and/or marginal illustrations depicting the flora, fauna, and natives of the lands shown in the map, often rendered with a high level of artistic skill. Visible in this detail from the much larger map, one of the inserted illustrations depicts two Native couples, one Montagnais and the other Almouchiquois. Although based on Champlain's descriptions, the engraver clearly modeled the facial features on Europeans (note the bearded man on the right). Yet the figures do illustrate the basic distinction Champlain drew between nomadic foragers and sedentary agricultural peoples (the Montagnais on the left are nomadic hunter-gatherers; the Almouchiquois on the right are semi-nomadic farmers). Europeans tended to divide the peoples they encountered into these fundamental categories. The costumes rendered here reflect Champlain's descriptions of Native dress and implements. Although Champlain had not yet reached Huronia, he shows the Great Lakes in this map based on information he had obtained from the Natives.

Samuel de Champlain, detail from Samuel de Champlain's map of 1612, plate lxxxi, in *The Works of Samuel de Champlain*, ed. Henry Percival Biggar et al. (Toronto: Champlain Society, 1922–1935; Toronto: University of Toronto Press, 1971).

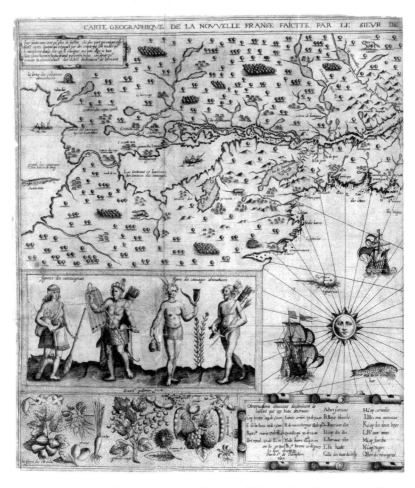

Detail of Champlain's 1612 map, with images of Native Americans and native plants.

6

SAMUEL DE CHAMPLAIN

On His Mapmaking Philosophy and Techniques

1613

This excerpt from Champlain's The Voyages of the Sieur de Champlain of Saintonge, Captain in the Ordinary for the King, in the Navy *(1613) offers a rare opportunity not only to examine one of his early maps but also to listen to the mapmaker explain the meaning of the map and some of the techniques he used to make it. To achieve the high levels of accuracy found in his maps, Champlain clearly took many more observations than he included in his works, and he was highly skilled in calculating latitude with an extraordinary level of accuracy given the relatively simple instruments he used. He also usually did a good job of estimating distance based on visual observation and information gleaned from the Natives with whom he discussed geography at length. He relied on the most scientific methods of his day for calculating longitude and determining compass declinations, and his errors are primarily the result of the science of his time—the limited knowledge about magnetic variation and the lack of a clock with the accuracy necessary to calculate longitude.*

Champlain also compares this map with the much larger 1612 map of New France (Document 5) that he made during the same period (both were included in his The Voyages, *which was published in 1613). He designed this map to be of use especially to navigators and explorers, whereas he created the larger 1612 map primarily for use by general readers of* The Voyages. *Thus the 1613 map depicts much more of the interior than Champlain's earlier 1607 map (Document 4), which covered much of the same ground as this one but predates his expeditions up the Ottawa River and to the Great Lakes.*

Samuel de Champlain, *The Voyages of the Sieur de Champlain of Saintonge, Captain in the Ordinary for the King in the Navy* (1613), vol. 2, bk. 2, "The Third Voyage of the Sieur de Champlain in the Year 1611," trans. J. Squair, in *The Works of Samuel de Champlain,* ed. Henry Percival Biggar et al. (Toronto: Champlain Society, 1922–1935; Toronto: University of Toronto Press, 1971), 222–27.

Explanation of the Two Maps of New France[1]

It has seemed to me a good thing to write something also regarding the two maps, in order to explain these; for although one is the counterpart of the other, as far as the harbours, bays, capes, headlands, and courses of the rivers are concerned, they differ with respect to their orientations. The smaller one is in its true meridian according to what the Sieur de Castelfranc [Guillaume de Nautonier] shows this to be in his book on the *Mecometry of the Compass* [1603], wherein I have taken note of several variations which have been of great service to me, as will be seen on the said map, along with all the altitudes, latitudes and longitudes from the forty-first as far as the fifty-first degree of latitude north. These constitute the limits of Canada, or Grand Bay [gulf of the Saint Lawrence], where the Basques and Spaniards usually carry on their whale fishing. I have also noted the variation at certain places on the great river St. Lawrence in latitude 45°, where it reaches as much as 21°, which is the greatest that I have observed. And this little map can very well be used for navigation, provided one knows how to adjust the needle to the compass-card.[2] If, for example, I wish to use this, it is necessary for greater facility to take a compass-card on which the thirty-two points are equally marked, and to place the needle twelve, fifteen, or sixteen degrees toward the north-west, which is about a point and a half, or a little more than north by west, and to place the card in the compass when you are on the Grand Bank, where the green fishery is carried on. By this means you can with great certainty find your way to all capes, harbours and rivers. I know there will be many who will be unwilling to make use of it, and will rather have recourse to the larger one, since it is drawn according to the compass of France, where the needle points north-east, and they have learned this method so well that it is difficult

---

[1] The "two maps" Champlain refers to are the 1612 map reproduced in Document 5 and the 1613 map reproduced with this document.

[2] The compass card had a wind rose containing rhumb lines. These were used for calculating wind direction and charting courses. Adjusting the needle was especially crucial because he was aware of what is called declination, or the angle between magnetic north, the point at which the northern axis of the earth's magnetic field points downward, and true north, the straight line from any particular spot on the globe and the geographic northern "pole" or axis of the earth. A compass needle will point toward magnetic rather than true north. This is not a problem when charting a course for a relatively short journey but causes serious errors when surveying or charting larger areas. Ideally an explorer would be able to calculate that angle to correct his course and to depict on his map the correspondence between his compass readings, which Champlain faithfully recorded, and their location on a map. Champlain's understanding of the problem put him in the forefront of early modern explorers in this respect, although he was often unsuccessful in making the necessary corrections on his maps.

to make them change. That is why I have drawn the large map in this way, for the satisfaction of the majority of the pilots and navigators to the coasts of New France, fearing lest, had I not made it so, they would have charged me with an error they would not have been able to explain. For nearly all of the small charts or maps of Newfoundland differ in the positions and altitudes of the coast. And if there are a few who possess some small specimens that are pretty correct, they consider them so valuable that they give no information about them to their own countrymen, who might derive some advantage from them. Now the small maps are made in such a way that their meridian line runs north-north-east, and their west-north-west becomes west, a thing contrary to the true meridian of this region, to call north-north-east, the north. For instead of the needle being taken to point north-west, it is taken to point north-east, as if we were in France. This has caused the error which has resulted and which will continue, since they hold this old custom from ancient times, and retain it, although they fall thereby into gross errors. They also use a compass set north and south, that is to say with the point of the needle under the *fleur-de-lis* [showing north]. It is by this compass that many draw their small maps which seems to me the best method, and to approach nearer to the true meridian of New France than do the compasses of eastern France which point north-east. It happened then in this way that the early navigators to western New France thought they would not be any more astray in going to those parts than in going to the Azores or to other places near to France, where the error in navigation is almost imperceptible, and where the pilots have no other compasses than those of France, which point north-east and show the true meridian. And sailing constantly towards the west, wishing to reach a certain point, they steered due west by their compass, thinking they were sailing along a parallel to the place they wished to reach. And sailing continuously in a straight line on the flat, and not on a circle, as all the parallels on the terrestrial globe run, having gone a long distance, and when nearly within sight of land, they sometimes found themselves three, four, or five degrees farther south than need be, and consequently were out in their latitude and reckoning. However, it is quite true that when fine weather came, and the sun appeared, they used to correct the error in their latitude, but not without wondering why their course was wrong, which was due to the fact that instead of sailing on a circle like the said parallel, they sailed in a straight line as on a flat surface, and that as the meridian changed, the points of the compass also changed, and consequently their course. It is therefore most necessary to know the meridian and the variation of the needle; for this may be of use to all

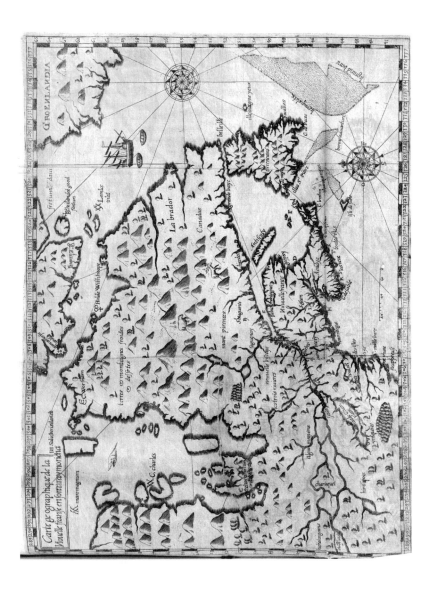

pilots who sail about the world; for should they be ignorant of it, particularly in the northern and southern latitudes, where the variations of the needle are greater, and moreover the circles of longitude shorter, the error would be greater through ignorance of the variation of the magnetic needle. That is how this error has arisen, and travellers not wishing or not knowing how to correct it, have left it as it now is, wherefore it is difficult to get rid of this common method of navigating in these said parts of New France. This is what led me to make this large map, both to give more detail than in the small one, as well as for the satisfaction of sailors who will be able to navigate as if it were by their own small maps or charts. And they will pardon me if I have not made them better and in greater detail; for the life of a man would not suffice to observe things so carefully that after the lapse of time some omission should not be found. The result will be that every observant and diligent person will be able when travelling to note things which are not marked on the map and to place them upon it. So much so, that in time no one will have any uncertainty about those parts. At least it seems to me that I have done my duty so far as I have been able, in not omitting to put into my map anything I have seen, nor to give the public detailed information upon what had never been discovered, or described in such detail as I have given. Although others in the past may have written about them, still it was very little compared with what we have discovered during the last ten years.

Opposite: Champlain's Map of 1613.
This map incorporates both Champlain's exploration of Lake Champlain but also information he gleaned from Natives regarding the existence and general contours of Hudson's Bay. Note the wind roses placed offshore on the map. These were decorative but also used for determining wind direction and charting a course. They are similar to the "compass-card" lines mentioned in the text.

7

SAMUEL DE CHAMPLAIN

On the Duties and Skills of a Good Seaman
1632

Although Champlain never had independent command of a large naval vessel, it is clear that from his earliest experiences with his father in Brouage and sailing first with his uncle, the Capitaine Provençal, and then with the Spanish fleet that sailed to the West Indies, he had learned much about seamanship and navigation. He evidently had both Spanish and French training in mapmaking, evidenced by, among other things, his use of the Spanish league to measure nautical miles and the usage of French surveying techniques when mapping inland areas and settlements. He had read the most advanced navigational treatise of his day, Pedro de Medina's Arte de navegar *(1554), which had been translated into French.* Treatise on Seamanship and the Duty of a Good Seaman *is useful not only because it displays Champlain's knowledge of seamanship and navigation, but also because it explains his philosophy of leadership, which seemed to have been modeled on that of a dutiful sea captain administrating a well-run vessel.*

It has appeared to me not inappropriate to compose a short treatise on what is requisite in order to be a good and finished navigator, and on the qualifications such a one should possess; he should above all be an upright, God-fearing man, not allowing God's holy name to be blasphemed on his ship, for fear, since he often finds himself in danger, lest His divine Majesty should punish him; and being careful night and morning above all else to have prayers offered up; and if the navigator can find means, I advise him to take with him a resourceful and competent priest or friar to give exhortations from time to time to the soldiers and sailors, so as to keep them always in the fear of God, and likewise to help them and take their confessions when they are sick, or in other

Samuel de Champlain, *Treatise on Seamanship and the Duty of a Good Seaman* (1632), vol. 6, trans. H. H. Langton, in *The Works of Samuel de Champlain*, ed. Henry Percival Biggar et al. (Toronto: Champlain Society, 1922–1935; Toronto: University of Toronto Press, 1971), 257–85.

ways to comfort them during the dangers encountered in the chances of the sea.

He [*i.e.*, the seaman or ship's master] should not be dainty about his eating, nor about his drink, adapting himself to the localities in which he finds himself. If he is dainty or of weak constitution, being exposed to variations of climate and diet he is liable to many ailments when making the change from wholesome to coarser food, such as is eaten at sea, which produces a condition of the blood quite opposed to his temperament. Such persons ought to be especially on their guard against scurvy more than others, who are also attacked by these tedious illnesses [*or*, diseases peculiar to long voyages]; and there should be some store of special remedies for those stricken by them.

[The good shipmaster] should be robust and alert, with good sea-legs, inured to hardships and toil, so that whatever happen he may be able to remain on deck, and in a strong voice give everybody orders what to do. Sometimes he must not be above lending a hand to the work himself, in order to make the sailors more prompt in their attention and to prevent confusion. He should be the only one to speak, lest differing orders, especially in situations where there may be doubt, cause the execution of one manoeuvre instead of another.

He should be pleasant and affable in conversation, authoritative in his orders, not too ready to talk with his fellows, except with those who share the command; otherwise in course of time a feeling of contempt for him might arise. He should also punish evil-doers severely, and make much of the good men, being kind to them, and at times gratifying them with some friendly demonstration, praising them, but not neglecting the others, so as not to give occasion for envy, which is often the source of bad feeling, a kind of gangrene which little by little corrupts and destroys the body; and want of early attention to this sometimes leads to conspiracies, divisions, or factions, which frequently cause the failure of the most promising undertakings. . . .

He should not allow himself to be overcome by wine; for when a captain or a seaman is a drunkard it is not very safe to entrust him with command or control, on account of the mischances that may result while he is sleeping like a pig, or has lost all sense and discretion and by reason of his drunkenness persists in insolence just when it is a matter of necessity to find some way of escape from the danger. . . .

The wise and cautious mariner ought not to trust too fully to his own judgment, when the pressing need is to take some important step or to deviate from a dangerous course. Let him take counsel with those whom he recognizes as the most sagacious, and particularly with old navigators who have had most experience of disasters at sea and have escaped from dangers and perils, and let him weigh well the reasons they may advance; for it is not often that one head holds everything, and, as the saying is, experience is better than knowledge. . . .

He must be cognizant, not ignorant, of everything that concerns the handling of the ship, everything at least that is necessary for putting to sea, and for mooring in readiness to sail, as well as all other matters needful for the safety of the ship.

He should take good care to have wholesome food and drink for his voyage and such as will keep well, to have good dry bins in which to keep the bread or biscuit, and especially on long voyages, and to have too much rather than too little; for sea-voyages are made only according as the weather is fair or foul and the winds [favourable or] contrary. He must be a good manager in serving out rations, giving each man what he reasonably needs; otherwise dissatisfaction is sometimes bred among sailors and soldiers when the latter are badly treated, and at such a time they are capable of doing more harm than good. He should entrust the serving out of rations to a good trustworthy commissary, no drunkard, but a provident fellow; for it is impossible to set too great store on a careful man in an office of this kind.

He should be particularly careful to see that everything is in good order on his ship, both to make it strong enough to support the weight of the guns it may mount, and to improve its appearance, so that he may take pleasure in it when he comes on board and when he leaves, and may please those who see him with his equipment about him, just as an architect is pleased when he has adorned the structure of a splendid building of his own designing. Everything on the ship should be very neat and clean, after the fashion of the Flemings, who commonly take first place in this respect over all the [other] seafaring nations.

He should take great pains when there are sailors and soldiers [together] to make them keep as clean as possible, and introduce such system that the soldiers are kept away from the sailors, so that there may be no confusion on the ship when from time to time they come to take part in a skirmish; and he should often have the space between decks cleansed of the filth that accumulates there; for it frequently causes a stench and gives rise to deadly disease, as if it were an infectious plague.

Before embarking he must have everything requisite for giving necessary aid to the men, together with one or two good surgeons who are not ignoramuses, like most of those who go to sea.

If possible, he must know his ship and have sailed her, or he must learn about her to know how she trims, and what speed she can make in twenty-four hours according to the strength of the winds, and what leeway she makes with the wind abeam, or when close-hauled with only the mainsail to steady her, so as not to labour and in order to keep more into the wind.

He must be apprehensive of finding himself in ordinary dangers, be it by accident or sometimes through ignorance or rashness involving you in them, as when you run before a wind in shore, [or] doggedly try to double a cape, or pursue a dangerous course by night among sandbanks, shoals, reefs, islands, rocks, or ice. But when ill-fortune brings you to such a pass, there you must display manly courage, make light of death though it confronts you, and in a steady voice and with cheery resolution urge all to take courage and do what can be done to escape the danger, and thus dispel fear from the most cowardly bosoms; for when they find themselves in a hazardous situation, every one looks to the man who is thought to have experience; for if he is seen to blanch and give his orders in a trembling and uncertain voice, all the others lose courage, and it is often seen that ships are lost in situations from which they might have got clear away if the men had seen their captain undaunted and determined, giving his orders boldly and with authority. . . .

He should be careful to take the ship's reckoning, to know its starting-point, its destination, its position, where the land lies in relation to it, on what quarter [*or*, rhumb of the wind]; he should know what leeway it makes, and what it gains on its course. He should not grow slack in taking account of these things, which is a main source of errors, and for this reason, in all changes of wind and course he should take great care to make certain of his position as nearly as possible, for sometimes good pilots are found to be quite out in their reckonings.

He should be a good navigator [of the high seas], skilled in taking the altitude either with the cross-staff or the astrolabe. He should know the right ascension of the sun, and what is its daily declination, in order to add or subtract.

Also [he should be able] to take the altitude of the pole-star with the cross-staff, take the bearing of the Guards, and add to or subtract from it the degrees that [they] are above or below the pole-star, according to the locality.

He should be able to recognize the Southern Cross when in south latitudes, add or subtract the degrees, recognize on occasion other stars if possible, so as to take their altitude when he loses sight of the former, or when he has not been able to take the sun's altitude owing to not seeing it exactly at noon.

He should know if the instruments he uses are accurate and properly made, and, in case of necessity, be able to construct others for his use.

He should be experienced in pricking the chart correctly, he should know if it is accurate according to the meridian where he is, and if he can rely upon it, [and] how many leagues for each point he must reckon for every higher degree. He should know the currents and tides, and where they are to be met with, so as to be able to make with certainty the harbours and other places which he has to visit, whether by day or night; and, if necessary for the purpose, he should be provided with good compasses and rutters for that object, and have seamen on the ship who know how to use them, if by chance he has not himself been there; for sometimes the lives of the whole ship's company are saved by making use of these in due time and place.

He should always be provided with plenty of good compasses, especially for long voyages; and for these he should have compass-cards which give easterly and westerly variation of the meridian line besides others giving north and south; and have a number of hour-glasses, and other instruments to the purpose.

He must know how to estimate the variations of the magnetic needle, in order to make allowance for them at the proper time and place, [how] to ascertain if the needles are properly magnetized and well balanced on the pivot, the gin-block straight, the gimbals free, and [how] if everything is not right, to put it in order; and for this purpose he should have a good loadstone, no matter what it may cost, [and] remove all iron from the vicinity of the compasses and binnacles, for much harm is done thereby. . . .

He must not forget frequently to acquaint himself with the variations of the compass needle in all localities, that is, to ascertain how much it varies from the meridian towards the east or west, which is useful in determining longitudes if one has observations for them; and when you return to the same place where you took them, and find the same variation, you would know whereabouts you are, whether it be in the hemisphere of Asia or that of Peru; and of this you should not be neglectful. It is also useful for finding the longitude of the locality, and for checking the wind directions according to the position of the ship, that is to say, all the names of the points of the mariner's compass.

He should know how to make charts, so as to be able to recognize accurately the lie of the coast, the entrances to ports, the harbours, roadsteads, rocks, shoals, reefs, islands, anchorages, capes, tide currents, inlets, rivers and streams, with their heights and depths, the buoys and beacons on the edges of shoals, and to describe the richness and fertility of the coast-lands, what they are fit for and what they can be expected to produce; also the native inhabitants of the localities, their laws and customs; and to make pictures of the birds, animals, fishes, plants, fruits, roots, trees, and everything unusual that is seen; for this a little skill in drawing is very necessary, and the art should be practised.

He must know the difference of longitude between two places, not only along one parallel but along them all, and even the difference for those places which are on different degrees of latitude, as from Rome to the Straits of Gibraltar, and similarly for all other places in the world.

He must know the Golden Number, the concurrent days of the year, the solar cycle, the dominical letter for each year, whether it is bissextile or not, the days on which the moon is in conjunction; on what days the months begin, how many days there are in each; the difference between the lunar and the solar year; the moon's age, how many degrees it traverses every day; what are the constellations of each month; how many leagues go to a degree, north and south; how long the days are for each parallel of latitude, and how much shorter or longer they become every day; what are the hours of sunset and sunrise; what is the sun's daily declination, whether in the northern or the southern hemisphere; and what days bring in the movable feasts.

He should know what is meant by a sphere, and its axis, the horizon, the meridian, the altitude, the equinoctial line, the tropics, the zodiac, parallels, longitude, latitude, the zenith, the centre, the arctic and antarctic circles, the poles, the northern and southern hemispheres, and other matters pertaining to the sphere, the names of the constellations and of the planets, and their motions.

He should know something about the regions, kingdoms, towns, cities, countries, islands, seas, and similar peculiarities of the land, something about their latitudes, longitudes and compass-variations if possible, and chiefly along the coasts where navigation should be conducted; and if he knows all this by experience as well as in theory, I think he may be classed among first-rate navigators.

Besides what is said above, a good sea-captain ought not to forget anything necessary [to be done] in a sea-fight, in which he may often find himself engaged. He should be brave, foreseeing, prudent, governed by good sound judgment, taking every advantage he can think of, whether for attack or defence, and if possible keep to windward of his enemy. For everyone knows how useful it is to have this advantage, whether for closing in or not; for the smoke of the gun-fire or of the fire-balls sometimes clouds the enemy so closely as to cause them confusion, preventing them from seeing what they ought to be doing. This is often the case in sea-fights.

The Captain should see in advance that all the guns and stone-mortars, the cannon-balls, fire-balls, powder, and other weapons needed for a fight or for protection are in good condition, handled and managed by men of sense and experience, so as to avoid the accidents which might happen, and particularly in respect of the powder and fire-balls. He should not put them in charge of any but discreet and understanding men, who know how to distribute them and make use of them to good purpose. He should see that such system is applied to all these matters that every man obeys his orders, whether it be for beating to quarters as ordered, or for handling the rigging, so that when each man is in his place, he does not leave it except by order of the commander, or of some one on his authority; and to this end all the sailors and seamen should be in readiness and prepared to have an eye to the rigging and sails, and to make them quite fast both at the foot and the head. The pilots should also be careful about matters connected with the steering and with those at the wheel. So also all the carpenters and caulkers, with their tools, must be ready to repair the damage that the enemy might do during a fight. The ship must not be encumbered, so that they may be able freely to go into the hold and repair the damage that the [enemy's] guns may do below the water-line. There should be vessels ready, filled with water to extinguish fire, in case some accident should happen, whether by effect of powder or fire-balls, or anything else.

He must see that the wounded are attended to promptly by those appointed for the purpose, and that the surgeons and some assistants are in readiness and provided with all their necessary instruments, as well as with medicaments and dressings, with fire in an iron brazier whether for cauterizing, or for anything else when necessity calls for it.

The commander must be always on the alert, sometimes in one place, sometimes in another, so as to encourage every man in doing his duty, and to make such dispositions that there shall be no confusion, since under all circumstances this [want of order] is the cause of great harm, and especially in a sea-fight. A wise and vigilant captain should take into consideration everything that makes for his advantage, and get the opinion of the most experienced men, so as to carry it out with the means he judges to be necessary and advantageous. He should not be a novice in encounters and their consequences, but should have had experience in the ordering of battles, which are fought in various modes of attack and assault, and in other matters which, experience shows, vary in the degree of their utility.

3

Witness to the Native American World

8

SAMUEL DE CHAMPLAIN

Renewing a Crucial Alliance between the French and the Montagnais

May 1603

The meeting between the French and the Natives at Tadoussac — described in this excerpt from Champlain's Of Savages *— took place in late May 1603 during Champlain's first voyage to New France. The French arrived at Tadoussac, the fur-trading post on the Saint Lawrence River, just as a group of Natives consisting of Montagnais, Etchemins, and Algonquins were celebrating a victory over their joint enemy, the Iroquois, who were based south of Lake Ontario. The Etchemins, also called Malecites or Penobscots, inhabited the region north and east of the Penobscot River in Maine (see Document 1), whereas the Natives called "Algonquins" here were the Ottawa (see Document 2). The Montagnais controlled the territory on both sides of the Saguenay River and had established a trading center at Tadoussac where the French had for decades come to purchase furs. The Montagnais, Ottawa, and Etchemins had formed an alliance against their mutual enemy, the Iroquois confederacy, which was based south of Lake Ontario and between Lake Ontario and Lake Champlain. The struggle was essentially over control of the supply of furs being sold to the French.*

Samuel de Champlain, *Of Savages, or Voyage of Samuel Champlain of Brouage, Made to New France in the Year 1603* (1603), vol. 1, trans. H. H. Langton, in *The Works of Samuel de Champlain*, ed. Henry Percival Biggar et al. (Toronto: Champlain Society, 1922–1935; Toronto: University of Toronto Press, 1971), 98–106.

During the tabagie *(probably derived from a Native word for feast)*
described here, Anadabijou, the tribal chief of the Montagnais, offered to
renew his alliance with the French. In return for French aid against the
Iroquois, the Montagnais and their allies promised to allow the French
to build settlements and trade furs in their territory. François Gravé,
Sieur du Pont (often simply referred to as "Pont-Gravé"), the leader of
the French expedition, agreed, and the alliance they sealed that day after
smoking tobacco in "peace pipes" endured until the end of New France.
It also laid the foundation for future conflict between the French and the
powerful Iroquois confederacy, although conflict most likely would have
broken out between the French and the Iroquois in the long run anyway
due to competition for control of the fur trade.

On the twenty-seventh, accompanied by the two savages whom Monsieur du Pont brought to make report of what they had seen in France, and of the good reception the King had given them, we sought the savages at St. Matthew's point, which is a league from Tadoussac. As soon as we had landed we went to the lodge of their grand Sagamore, named Anadabijou, where we found him and some eighty or a hundred of his companions, making *Tabagie* (that is to say, a feast). He received us very well, after the fashion of the country, and made us sit down beside him, while all the savages ranged themselves one next the other on both sides of the lodge. One of the savages whom we had brought began to make his oration, of the good reception that the king had given them, and of the good entertainment they had received in France, and that they might feel assured His Majesty wished them well, and desired to people their country, and to make peace with their enemies (who are the Iroquois) or send forces to vanquish them. He also told of the fine castles, palaces, houses, and peoples they had seen, and of our manner of living. He was heard with the greatest possible silence. Now when he had ended his oration, the said grand Sagamore Anadabijou, who had listened to him attentively, began to smoke tobacco, and to pass on his pipe to Monsieur du Pont-Gravé of St. Malo, and to me, and to certain other Sagamores who were near him. After smoking some time, he began to address the whole gathering, speaking with gravity, pausing sometimes a little, and then resuming his speech, saying to them, that in truth they ought to be very glad to have His Majesty for their great friend. They answered all with one voice, *Ho, ho, ho*, which is to say, *yes, yes*. Continuing his speech, he said that he was well content that His said

Majesty should people their country, and make war on their enemies, and that there was no nation in the world to which they wished more good than to the French. Finally, he gave them all to understand the advantage and profit they might receive from His said Majesty. When he had ended his speech, we went out of his lodge, and they began to hold their *Tabagie* or feast, which they make with the flesh of moose, which is like beef, with that of bear, seal, and beaver, which are their most ordinary meats, and with great quantities of wild fowl. They had eight or ten kettles full of meats in the midst of the said lodge, and these were set some six paces apart, and each on its own fire. The men sat on both sides (as I said before), each with his porringer made of the bark of a tree; and when the meat is cooked, one of them apportions to every man his part, into these dishes, out of which they feed very filthily, for when their hands are greasy they rub them on their hair, or else on the hair of their dogs, of which they have many for hunting. Before their meat was cooked, one of them rose up, and took a dog, and went leaping about the said kettles from one end of the lodge to the other. When he came in front of the grand Sagamore, he threw his dog violently upon the ground, and then all with one voice cried, *Ho, ho, ho*; having done this, he went and sat down in his place. Immediately another rose up and did the like, and so they continued until the meat was cooked. Then when they had ended their feast, they began to dance, taking in their hands as a mark of rejoicing the scalps of their enemies, which hung behind them. There were one or two who sang, keeping time by the beat of their hands, which they strike upon their knees; then they stop sometimes, and cry, *Ho, ho, ho*, and begin again to dance, panting like a man out of breath. They were celebrating this triumph for a victory they had won over the Iroquois, of whom they had slain about a hundred, whose scalps they cut off, and had with them for the ceremony. Three nations had taken part in the war, the Etechemins, Algonquins, and Montagnais, to the number of a thousand, and these went on the war-path against the Iroquois, whom they encountered at the mouth of the river of the Iroquois [the Richelieu River] and slew a hundred of them. The mode of warfare which they practise is altogether by surprises; for otherwise they would be afraid, and too much in dread of the said Iroquois, who are in greater number than the said Montagnais, Etechemins, and Algonquins.

On the twenty-eighth day of this month, they came and encamped at the aforesaid harbour of Tadoussac, where lay our ship. At daybreak their grand Sagamore came out of his lodge, going round about all the other lodges, and crying with a loud voice that they should break camp to go to Tadoussac, where their good friends were. Immediately every man in a trice [speedily] took down his lodge, and the said grand Captain was the first to begin to take his canoe and carry it to the water, wherein he embarked his wife and children, and a quantity of furs; and in like manner were launched well nigh two hundred canoes, which go extraordinarily well; for though our shallop [small sailboat] was well manned, yet they went more swiftly than we. There are but two that paddle, the man and the wife. Their canoes are some eight or nine paces long, and a pace or a pace and a half broad amidships, and grow sharper and sharper toward both ends. They are very liable to overturn, if one know not how to manage them rightly; for they are made of a bark of trees called birch-bark, strengthened within by little circles of wood strongly and neatly fashioned, and are so light that a man can carry one of them easily; and every canoe can carry the weight of a pipe [about 100 gallons]. When they wish to go overland to get to some river where they have business, they carry them with them.

Their lodges are low, made like tents, covered with the aforesaid tree-bark; they leave all the top uncovered about a foot space, through which the light comes in; and make many fires right in the midst of their lodge, where there are sometimes ten households together. They sleep upon skins one beside another, and their dogs with them.

They were in number about a thousand persons, men as well as women and children. The spot at St. Matthew's point, where they were first encamped, is very pretty. They were at the bottom of a little hill, covered with fir and cypress trees. Upon this point there is a little level plot, which is visible from afar off, and upon the top of the hill is a level plain, a league long, and half a league broad, covered with trees; the soil is very sandy, and there is good pasture there. All the rest is nothing but mountains of very barren rocks. The sea beats round about the said hill, which is dry almost for a full half league at low water.

9

SAMUEL DE CHAMPLAIN

Observations and Mutual Incomprehension at Tadoussac

1603

After the feast and negotiations described in Document 8, Champlain remained at Tadoussac for several days observing and chatting with the Montagnais, Etchemins, and Ottawa prior to launching further explorations with Native guides up the Saint Lawrence River. From these passages it is evident that Champlain was keenly interested in the Natives, their lifestyle, and their beliefs. But it is also clear that Champlain was unable to fully comprehend the meaning of most of the Native behavior he witnessed or Native discourses he heard (in translation). As a result, he frequently misinterpreted the words and actions of the Natives, in particular when he described their religious ceremonies and rituals. Like most Europeans, Champlain mistakenly describes Native rituals, focused as they were on communication with the spirit world through dreams and trances, as a form of devil worship.

On the ninth day of June the savages all began to make merry together, and to hold their feast, as I have described before, and to dance, in honour of the aforesaid victory which they had obtained over their enemies. Now after they had made good cheer, the Algonquins, one of the three nations, went out of their lodges, and withdrew by themselves into an open place. Here they arranged all their women and girls side by side, and themselves stood behind, singing all in unison in the manner I have already described. Suddenly all the women and girls proceeded to cast off their mantles of skins, and stripped themselves stark naked, showing their privities, but retaining their ornaments of matachias, which are beads and braided cords made of porcupine quills, dyed of various

Samuel de Champlain, *Of Savages, or Voyage of Samuel Champlain of Brouage, Made to New France in the Year 1603* (1603), vol. 1, trans. H. H. Langton, in *The Works of Samuel de Champlain*, ed. Henry Percival Biggar et al. (Toronto: Champlain Society, 1922–1935; Toronto: University of Toronto Press, 1971), 107–17.

colours. After they had made an end of their songs, they cried all with
one voice, *Ho, ho, ho*; at the same instant all the women and girls covered themselves with their mantles, which were at their feet, and they
had a short rest; then all at once beginning again to sing, they let fall
their mantles as before. They do not stir from one spot when they dance,
but make certain gestures and motions of the body, first lifting up one
foot and then the other, and stamping upon the ground. While they were
performing this dance, the Sagamore of the Algonquins, whose name
was Besouat, was seated before the said women and girls, between two
poles, on which hung the scalps of their enemies. Sometimes he arose
and moved away to address the Montagnais and Etechemins, saying
to them: "See how we rejoice for the victory which we have obtained
over our enemies; ye must do the like, that we may be satisfied." Then
all cried together, *Ho, ho, ho*. As soon as he had returned to his place,
the grand Sagamore and all his companions [Anadabijou and the Mon-
tagnais] cast off their mantles, being stark naked save their privities,
which were covered with a small piece of skin, and each of them took
what seemed proper to him, such as matachias, tomahawks, swords,
kettles, pieces of fat, moose flesh, seal; in a word, every one had a present, which they proceeded to give to the Algonquins. After all these ceremonies the dance came to an end, and the Algonquins, both men and
women, carried away their presents to their lodges. They also matched
two of the fittest men of each nation, whom they caused to run, and he
who was swiftest in the race had a present. . . .

They are for the most part a people that has no law, as far as I could
see and learn from the said grand Sagamore [Anadabijou], who told me
that in truth they believe there is a God, who has made all things. Then
I said to him, "Since they believe in one God only, how had He brought
them into the world, and whence had they come?" He answered me, that
after God had made all things, He took a number of arrows, and stuck
them in the ground, whence He drew men and women, which have mul-
tiplied in the world up to the present, and had their origin in this fashion.
I replied to him, that what he said was false; but that in truth there was
but one God, who had created all things on earth, and in the heavens.
Seeing all these things so perfect, without anybody to govern this world
beneath, He took the slime of the earth, and of it created Adam, our first
father. While Adam slept, God took a rib of the said Adam, and out of it
formed Eve, whom He gave him for his companion; and that it was the
truth that they and we had our origin after this manner, and not from
arrows as was their belief. He replied nothing, save that he approved
rather what I said, than that which he told me. I asked him also, whether

he did not believe there was more than one God. He replied that their belief was, that there was one God, one Son, one Mother, and the Sun, which were four; yet that God was above them all; but that the Son and the Sun were good, because of the benefit they received of them, but that the Mother was of no value, and ate them up, and that the Father was not very good. I showed him his error according to our faith, in which he manifested some small belief. I asked him whether they had not seen, or heard their ancestors tell that God had come into the world. He told me that he had not seen Him; but that in old time there were five men who went toward the setting sun and met God, who asked them, "Whither go ye?" They said, "We go in search of a living." God answered them, "You shall find it here." They went on without regard to what God had said to them: who took a stone, and touched two of them with it, and they were turned into stones. And He said again to the other three, "Whither go ye?" And they answered as at first: and God said to them again, "Go no further, you shall find it here." And seeing that nothing came to them, they went on: and God took two sticks, and touched the two first with them, and they were turned into sticks; and the fifth halted and would go no further. And God asked him again, "Whither goest thou?" "I go in search of my living." "Stay, and thou shalt find it." He stayed without going any further, and God gave him meat, and he ate it; after he had made good cheer, he returned among other savages, and told them all the above story.

He told me also, that once upon a time there was a man who had a good supply of tobacco (which is a herb, of which they take the smoke), and that God came to this man, and asked him where was his tobacco-pipe. The man took his tobacco-pipe and gave it to God, who smoked tobacco a great while: after He had smoked enough, God broke the said pipe into many pieces: and the man asked Him, "Why hast Thou broken my pipe? Surely Thou seest that I have no other." And God took one of His own, and gave it to him, saying to him: "Here is one that I give thee, carry it to thy grand Sagamore; charge him to keep it, and if he keep it well, he shall never want for anything whatever, nor any of his companions." The man took the pipe, and gave it to his grand Sagamore, and as long as he kept it the savages wanted for nothing in the world; but afterwards the said Sagamore lost this pipe, and this is the reason of the great famine which sometimes comes among them. I asked him whether he believed all this; and he said yes, and that it was true. Now I believe this is the reason why they say that God is not very good. But I replied and told him, that God was wholly good; and that without doubt it was the Devil who had appeared to those men, and that if they believed in God as we do, they should lack nothing of which they stood in need; that the sun which they beheld, the moon and the stars, had been created by this great God, who made heaven and earth; and that these have no power but that which God has given them; that we believe in this great God, who of His goodness had sent us His dear Son, who, being conceived by the Holy Ghost, became human flesh in the virginal womb of the Virgin Mary, lived thirty-three years on earth, working infinite miracles, raising up the dead, healing the sick, casting out devils, giving sight to the blind, teaching men the will of God His Father, in order to serve, honour, and worship Him; shed His blood, and suffered death and passion for us and for our sins, and redeemed mankind, and being buried rose again, descended into hell and ascended into heaven, where He sat on the right hand of God His Father. I told him this was the belief of all Christians, who believe in the Father, the Son, and the Holy Ghost, which nevertheless are not three Gods, but one same and one sole God, and a Trinity, in which is no before or after, no greater or less; that the Virgin Mary, the Mother of the Son of God, and all men and women who have lived in this world doing the commandments of God, and have suffered martyrdom for His name's sake, and who by God's permission have wrought miracles, and are saints in heaven in His Paradise, do all pray this great divine Majesty for us, to pardon us our faults and sins which we commit against His law and commandments. And so, by the prayers of the saints in heaven, and by our prayers which we offer to His divine Majesty, He gives us that which we need, and the Devil has no power over us, and can do us no harm; that if they had this belief, they should be as we, and the Devil would be unable to do them more harm, and they should lack nothing they required.

Thereupon the said Sagamore told me that he approved what I said. I asked him what ceremony they used in praying to their God. He told me, that they did not make much use of ceremonies, but that every one prayed in his heart as he thought good. This is why I believe they have no law among them, nor know what it is to worship and pray to God, and that most of them live like brute beasts; and I think they would speedily be brought to be good Christians, if their country were colonised, which most of them would like.

They have among them certain savages whom they call *Pilotoua*, who speak to the Devil face to face and he tells them what they must do, both in war and in other affairs; and if he should command them to put into execution any enterprise, either to kill a Frenchman or one of their own nation, they would immediately obey his command.

Moreover they believe that all the dreams they dream are true; and indeed there are many of them who say that they have seen in dreams things which happen or will happen. But to speak the truth about them, these are visions of the Devil, who deceives and misleads them. This is all their beliefs that I could learn from them, and they are brutish.

All these peoples are well proportioned in body, without any deformity; they are agile, and the women are well shapen, filled out and plump, of a swarthy colour on account of the profusion of a certain pigment with which they rub themselves, and which gives them an olive hue. They are clad in skins, one part of their bodies is covered, and the other part uncovered. But in winter they provide for the whole body; for they are clad with good furs, such as the skins of moose, otter, beavers, bears, seals, stags, and deer, which they have in abundance. In the winter when the snows are heavy they make a kind of racket twice or thrice as big as ours in France, which they fasten to their feet, and so walk on the snow without sinking; for otherwise they could not hunt nor make their way in many places.

They have also a kind of marriage, which is, that when a girl is fourteen or fifteen years old, she may have several suitors and friends, and keep company with all whom she likes: then at the end of some five or six years, she will take which of them she pleases for her husband, and they will live together thus to the end of their lives, unless after they have lived some time together they have no children, when the man may get a divorce and take another wife, saying that his own is worth nothing. Thus the girls are more free than the married women; but after they are married they are chaste, and their husbands for the most part are jealous, and these give presents to the father or kindred of the girl whom they have married. This is the ceremony and manner of their conduct in their marriages.

Touching their burials, when a man or woman dies, they make a pit, in which they put all the goods they have, such as kettles, furs, hatchets, bows and arrows, robes and other things, and then they place the body in the pit, and cover it with earth, and lay on top a great many large pieces of wood, and one stake they set up on end and paint it red on the upper part. They believe in the immortality of the soul, and say that when they die they go into other lands to make merry with their kindred and friends.

10

SAMUEL DE CHAMPLAIN

On the Founding of Québec, and Observations of the Montagnais Living Nearby

1608

In July 1608 Champlain set about creating a settlement at the site of what is now the Old Town section of Québec. He chose this location, about a hundred miles further up the Saint Lawrence River from Tadoussac, because the climate was warmer and the land flatter and more suited to agriculture. Even though Champlain knew that financially the French colonization effort in New France still depended on the profits from the fur trade, his personal vision was shifting from finding a Northwest Passage to establishing a durable agricultural colony. Champlain hoped that ultimately much of the labor force for New France would come from Natives who had been "civilized" by adopting a settled European agricultural lifestyle and, eventually, creating a new population, which would be French in culture, Catholic in religion, and ethnically mixed.

The Montagnais described in this section of The Voyages of the Sieur de Champlain of Saintonge, Captain in the Ordinary for the King in the Navy *(1613) were hunter-gatherers allied to the French. As Champlain supervised the establishment of the Québec settlement, therefore, he also observed closely the ways of the Montagnais who lived near the settlement and came often to trade with the French. Champlain distinguished carefully between nomadic societies mostly reliant on foraging, hunting, and fishing, such as the Montagnais and many Algonquian-speaking peoples living north of the Saint Lawrence River, and peoples such as the Huron (an Iroquoian-speaking people who lived near Georgian Bay) and the Iroquoian-speaking tribes of what is today upstate New York who practiced extensive agriculture and were settled most of the year. This distinction is depicted visually in Champlain's 1612 map (Document 5).*

Samuel de Champlain, *The Voyages of the Sieur de Champlain of Saintonge, Captain in the Ordinary for the King in the Navy* (1613), in vol. 2, bk. 2, trans. J. Squair, in *The Works of Samuel de Champlain*, ed. Henry Percival Biggar et al. (Toronto: Champlain Society, 1922–1935; Toronto: University of Toronto Press, 1971), 35–36, 44–51.

When all this was over, Pont-Gravé sailed from Quebec on September 18, to return to France with the three prisoners. After their departure the others all conducted themselves properly in their duty.

I continued the construction of our quarters, which contained three main buildings of two stories. Each one was three fathoms long and two and a half wide. The storehouse was six long and three wide, with a fine cellar six feet high. All the way round our buildings I had a gallery made, outside the second story, which was a very convenient thing. There were also ditches fifteen feet wide and six deep, and outside these I made several salients which enclosed a part of the buildings, and there we put our cannon. . . .

Whilst the carpenters, sawyers, and other workmen were busy at our quarters, I set all the rest to work clearing the land about our settlement in order to make gardens in which to sow grains and seed, for the purpose of seeing how the whole thing would succeed, particularly since the soil seemed to be very good.

Meanwhile many of the natives had encamped near us, who used to fish for eels, which begin to come up about September 15 and finish on October 15. During this time the natives all live upon this manna and dry some for the winter to last till the month of February, when the snow is two and a half or even three feet deep at the most. At that time when their eels and the other things which they dry are prepared, they go off beaver-hunting and remain away until the beginning of January. When they were engaged on this, they left in our keeping all their eels and other things till their return, which took place on December 15. And they told us that they did not take many beavers because the waters were too high, on account of the rivers overflowing. I gave them back all their provisions which only lasted them till January 20. When their eels give out they resort to hunting the moose and any other wild beasts they may find, until springtime, at which season I was able to furnish them with various supplies. I studied their customs very particularly.

All these tribes suffer so much from hunger that sometimes they are obliged to live on certain shell-fish, and to eat their dogs and the skins with which they clothe themselves against the cold. I consider that, if anyone were to show them how to live, and how to till the soil, and other things, they would learn very well; for there are many of them who have good judgment, and reply pointedly to the questions put to them. But they have bad points: they are revengeful and awful liars, people whom one must not trust too far, but rather judiciously, and with force in one's hand. They promise readily, but perform badly. They are people, the majority of whom, so far as I have been able to see, respect no law, but have plenty of false beliefs. I asked them what sort of ceremonies they used in praying to their God. They told me that they had no other than this, that each one prayed to God in his heart, just as it suited him. That is why there is no law amongst them, and that they do not know what it is to pray to and worship God, living as they do like brute beasts. I believe they would soon be brought to be good Christians, if one were to live in their country, as the majority of them desire. They have amongst them some natives whom they call *Pillotois* [shamans], who, they believe, speak to the devil[1] face to face, and he tells them what they must do in war as well as in other matters, and if he were to order them to put any enterprise into execution, they would at once obey his command. So, also, they believe that all their dreams are true, and indeed there are many of them who say they have had visions and dreamed things which came to pass, or will come to pass. But to tell the truth about these things, they are visions from the devil who deceives them and leads them astray. That is all I have been able to learn about their brutish beliefs. All these people are well-proportioned in body, without deformity, and are agile. The women are also well-formed, plump, and of a dusky hue, on account of certain colouring materials with which they rub themselves, which render them permanently olive-coloured. They are clothed in skins; a part of their bodies is covered, and the other part is bare. But in winter they are completely covered, for they are clad in good furs, such as the skins of moose, otter, beaver, bear, seal, deer (male and female), which are very numerous. In the winter when the snow is deep, they make a kind of racket, two or three times as large as those in France, and attach them to their feet, and with these they walk over the snow without sinking. Otherwise they could not hunt nor travel in many places.

They have also a sort of marriage, which is after this fashion. When a girl is fourteen or fifteen years of age and has several suitors, she keeps company with as many as she wishes. Then after five or six years she chooses the one she likes best for her husband, and they live together to the end of their lives, unless, after they have lived together for some time, the woman has no children, when the husband may divorce her and take another wife, alleging that his own is no good. In this way the girls have greater freedom than the women. After they are married they are chaste and their husbands are generally jealous, and they give

---

[1] Again, when Champlain uses the term *devil*, he is describing Native ceremonies designed to allow shamans to communicate directly with the spirit world. Like all Europeans of his day, Champlain assumed that the spirits with whom the shamans sought to communicate were devils.

presents to the fathers or relatives of the girls they have married. Such are the ceremonies and customs followed in their marriages.

As regards their burials, when a man or a woman dies, they make a grave, into which they put everything they own, such as kettles, furs, hatchets, bows, arrows, skins and other things. Then they put the body into the grave, and cover it with earth, and put many big pieces of wood on top, and set one piece on end and paint it red in the upper part. They believe in the immortality of souls, and say that the dead enjoy happiness in other lands with their relatives and friends who have died. In the case of chiefs, or others having influence, they hold a banquet after their death three times a year and sing and dance upon their grave.

The whole time they were with us, which was the safest place for them, they were in such constant dread of their enemies, that they often took fright at night in their dreams, and would send their wives and children to our fort, the gates of which I used to have opened for them, but let the men remain about the fort, not permitting them to enter; for they were as safe there as to their persons as if they had been inside. And I used to send out five or six of our men to give them courage, and to go and search the woods whether they could see anything, which used to satisfy them. They are very timid and fear their enemies greatly, and hardly ever sleep quietly wherever they are, although I reassured them every day as much as I could, by admonishing them to do as we did, that is to say that some of them should watch, whilst the others slept, and that each should have his arms ready like a sentinel on duty, and that they should not take dreams as truth upon which to rely, since most of them are only fables, with other considerations on the same subject. But these admonitions were of small avail, and they used to say that we knew better than they did how to protect ourselves in every way, and that in time if we were to come and live in their country they would be able to learn these.

11

SAMUEL DE CHAMPLAIN

A Journey into Iroquois Territory
and a Battle at Lake Champlain

1609

*To keep a promise Champlain had made to his Montagnais and Algon-
quin allies during previous voyages to the Saint Lawrence River, in July
1609 Champlain and two French soldiers accompanied a raiding party
up the Richelieu River and participated in an attack on an Iroquois out-
post near what is today Ticonderoga, New York. The Natives were interested in testing his courage and the strength of his vital spirit or energy
in battle so they could ascertain whether he would be a trustworthy and
useful ally. Champlain had several goals. He was always anxious to
explore new territory, and he also wanted to seal his alliance with the
Natives of New France, which he realized—sooner than most of his com-
patriots—depended on demonstrating a willingness to aid them against
their Native foes. These were the terms that his allies had demanded
of him.*

*In participating in the raid Champlain became the first European
to journey beyond the rapids on the Richelieu River and to explore Lake
Champlain. We see in this passage from* The Voyages of the Sieur de
Champlain of Saintonge, Captain in the Ordinary for the King in the
Navy *his careful attention to the landscape, flora, and fauna, as well as
to the customs, behavior, and mentality of his Native allies. Always Euro-
centric, Champlain professed his puzzlement at their war strategies and
their reliance on dreams at least as much as on reconnaissance to deter-
mine the place and time to commence hostilities. His critique of course
also helped to emphasize to his French readers why the Native victory in
this case resulted, according to Champlain, from his decisive intervention
in the battle.*

Samuel de Champlain, *The Voyages of the Sieur de Champlain of Saintonge, Captain in the
Ordinary for the King in the Navy* (1613) with *Defeat of the Iroquois at Lake Champlain,*
plate v, vol. 2, bk. 2, trans. J. Squair, in *The Works of Samuel de Champlain,* ed. Henry
Percival Biggar et al. (Toronto: Champlain Society, 1922–1935; Toronto: University of
Toronto Press, 1971), 82–101.

I set out then from the rapid of the river of the Iroquois on the second of July [1609]. All the Indians began to carry their canoes, arms and baggage about half a league by land, to avoid the swiftness and force of the rapid. This they soon accomplished.

Then they put all the canoes into the water and two men with their baggage into each; but they made one of the men of each canoe go by land some three leagues which is about the length of the rapids, but the water is here less impetuous than at the entrance, except in certain places where rocks block the river, which is only some three or four hundred yards wide. After we had passed the rapids, which was not without difficulty, all the Indians who had gone overland, by a rather pleasant path through level country, although there were many trees, again got into their canoes. The men whom I had with me also went by land, but I went by water in a canoe. The Indians held a review of all their people and there were sixty men in twenty-four canoes. After holding the review we kept on our way as far as an island, three leagues long, which was covered with the most beautiful pines I had ever seen. There the Indians hunted and took some game. Continuing some three leagues farther, we encamped to take rest during the following night.

Immediately each began, some to cut down trees, others to strip bark from the trees to cover their wigwams in which to take shelter, others to fell big trees for a barricade on the bank of the river round their wigwams. They know how to do this so quickly that after less than two hours' work, five hundred of their enemies would have had difficulty in driving them out, without losing many men. They do not barricade the river bank where their boats are drawn up, in order to embark in case of need. After their wigwams had been set up, according to their custom each time they camp, they sent three canoes with nine good men, to reconnoitre two or three leagues ahead, whether they could perceive anything; and afterwards these retired. All night long they rely upon the explorations of these scouts, and it is a very bad custom; for sometimes they are surprised in their sleep by their enemies, who club them before they have time to rise and defend themselves. Realizing this, I pointed out to them the mistake they were making and said that they ought to keep watch as they had seen us do every night, and have men posted to listen and see whether they might perceive anything, and not live as they were doing like silly creatures. They told me that they could not stay awake, and that they worked enough during the day when hunting. Besides when they go to war they divide their men into three troops, that is, one troop for hunting, scattered in various directions, another troop which forms the bulk of their men is always under arms, and the other troop of scouts to reconnoitre along the rivers and see whether there is any mark or sign to show where their enemies or their friends have gone. This they know by certain marks by which the chiefs of one nation designate those of another, notifying one another from time to time of any variations of these. In this way they recognise whether enemies or friends have passed that way. The hunters never hunt in advance of the main body, nor of the scouts, in order not to give alarm or to cause confusion, but only when these have retired and in a direction from which they do not expect the enemy. They go on in this way until they are within two or three days' march of their enemy, when they proceed stealthily by night, all in a body, except the scouts. In the day time they retire into the thick of the woods, where they rest without any straggling, or making a noise, or making a fire even for the purpose of cooking. And this they do so as not to be noticed, if by chance their enemy should pass that way. The only light they make is for the purpose of smoking which is almost nothing. They eat baked Indian meal, steeped in water, which becomes like porridge. They keep these meal cakes for their needs, when they are near the enemy or when they are retiring after an attack; for then they do not waste time in hunting but retire quickly.

Each time they encamp they have their *Pilotois* or *Ostemoy* who are people who play the part of wizards, in whom these tribes have confidence. One of these wizards will set up a tent, surround it with small trees, and cover it with his beaver-skin. When it is made, he gets inside so that he is completely hidden; then he seizes one of the poles of his tent and shakes it whilst he mumbles between his teeth certain words, with which he declares he is invoking the devil, who appears to him in the form of a stone and tells him whether his friends will come upon their enemies and kill many of them. This *Pilotois* will lie flat on the ground, without moving, merely speaking to the devil, and suddenly he will rise to his feet, speaking and writhing so that he is all in a perspiration, although stark naked. The whole tribe will be about the tent sitting on their buttocks like monkeys. They often told me that the shaking of the tent which I saw, was caused by the devil and not by the man inside, although I saw the contrary; for, as I have said above, it was the *Pilotois* who would seize one of the poles of the tent, and make it move in this way. They told me also that I should see fire coming out of the top, but I never saw any. These scamps also counterfeit a loud, distinct voice, and speak a language unknown to the other Indians. And when they speak in an old man's voice, the rest think that the devil is speaking, and is telling them what is going to happen in their war, and what they must do.

Yet out of a hundred words all these scoundrels, who pretend to be wizards, do not speak two that are true, and go on deceiving these poor people to get things from them, as do many others in this world who resemble these gentry. I often pointed out to them that what they did was pure folly, and that they ought not to believe in such things.

Having learned from their wizards what is to happen to them, the chiefs take sticks a foot long, one for each man, and indicate by others somewhat longer, their leaders. Then they go into the wood, and level off a place five or six feet square, where the headman, as sergeant-major, arranges all these sticks as to him seems best. Then he calls all his companions, who approach fully armed, and he shows them the rank and order which they are to observe when they fight with the enemy. This all these Indians regard attentively, and notice the figure made with these sticks by their chief. And afterwards they retire from that place and begin to arrange themselves in the order in which they have seen these sticks. Then they mix themselves up and again put themselves in proper order, repeating this two or three times, and go back to their camp, without any need of a sergeant to make them keep their ranks, which they are quite able to maintain without getting into confusion. Such is the method they observe on the war-path.

We departed on the following day, pursuing our way up the river as far as the entrance to the lake [Lake Champlain]. In it are many beautiful low islands covered with very fine woods and meadows with much wild fowl and animals to hunt, such as stags, fallow deer, fawns, roebucks, bears, and other kinds of animals which come from the mainland to these islands. We caught there a great many of them. There are also many beavers, both in that river and in several small streams which fall into it. This region although pleasant is not inhabited by Indians, on account of their wars; for they withdraw from the rivers as far as they can into the interior, in order not to be easily surprised.

On the following day we entered the lake which is some 80 or 100 leagues in length [Lake Champlain is about 125 miles long], in which I saw four beautiful islands about ten, twelve and fifteen leagues in length, which, like the Iroquois river, were formerly inhabited by Indians: but have been abandoned, since they have been at war with one another. There are also several rivers flowing into the lake, on whose banks are many fine trees of the same varieties we have in France, with many of the finest vines I had seen anywhere. There are many chestnut trees which I had only seen on the shore of this lake, in which there is also a great abundance of many species of fish. Amongst others there is one called by the natives *Chaousarou*, which is of various lengths; but the largest of them, as these tribes have told me, are from eight to ten feet long. I have seen some five feet long, which were as big as my thigh, and had a head as large as my two fists, with a snout two feet and a half long, and a double row of very sharp, dangerous teeth. Its body has a good deal the shape of the pike; but it is protected by scales of a silvery gray colour and so strong that a dagger could not pierce them. The end of its snout is like a pig's. This fish makes war on all the other fish which are in these lakes and rivers. And, according to what these tribes have told me, it shows marvellous ingenuity in that, when it wishes to catch birds, it goes in amongst the rushes or reeds which lie along the shores of the lake in several places, and puts its snout out of the water without moving. The result is that when the birds come and light on its snout, mistaking it for a stump of wood, the fish is so cunning that, shutting its half-open mouth, it pulls them by their feet under the water. The natives gave me the head of one of them, a thing they prize highly, saying that when they have a headache, they bleed themselves with the teeth of this fish at the spot where the pain is and it eases them at once.

Continuing our way along this lake in a westerly direction and viewing the country, I saw towards the east very high mountains on the tops of which there was snow.[1] I enquired of the natives whether these parts were inhabited. They said they were, and by the Iroquois, and that in those parts there were beautiful valleys and fields rich in corn such as I have eaten in that country, along with other products in abundance. And they said that the lake went close to the mountains, which, as I judged, might be some twenty-five leagues away from us. Towards the south I saw others which were not less lofty than the first-mentioned, but there was no snow on these [Adirondacks]. The Indians told me that it was there that we were to meet their enemies, that the mountains were thickly populated, and that we had to pass a rapid [at the site of Fort Ticonderoga] which I saw afterwards. Thence they said we had to enter another lake [Lake George] which is some nine or ten leagues in length, and that on reaching the end of it we had to go by land some two leagues and cross a river [Hudson] which descends to the coast of Norumbega [Maine coast], adjoining that of Florida. They could go there in their canoes in two days, as I learned afterwards from some prisoners we took, who conversed with me very particularly regarding all

---

[1] The climate of both Europe and North America during the seventeenth century was considerably colder than it is today, in part due to the effects of a pattern of worldwide cooling known as the Little Ice Age that extended from the thirteenth through the seventeenth centuries.

they knew, with the help of some Algonquin interpreters who knew the Iroquois language.

Now as we began to get within two or three days' journey of the home of their enemy, we proceeded only by night, and during the day we rested. Nevertheless, they kept up their usual superstitious ceremonies in order to know what was to happen to them in their undertakings, and often would come and ask me whether I had had dreams and had seen their enemies. I would tell them that I had not, but nevertheless continued to inspire them with courage and good hope. When night came on, we set off on our way until the next morning. Then we retired into the thick woods where we spent the rest of the day. Towards ten or eleven o'clock, after walking around our camp, I went to take a rest, and while asleep I dreamed that I saw in the lake near a mountain our enemies, the Iroquois, drowning before our eyes. I wanted to succour them, but our Indian allies said to me that we should let them all perish; for they were bad men. When I awoke they did not fail to ask me as usual whether I had dreamed anything. I told them what I had seen in my dream. This gave them such confidence that they no longer had any doubt as to the good fortune awaiting them.

Evening having come, we embarked in our canoes in order to proceed on our way, and as we were paddling along very quietly, and without making any noise, about ten o'clock at night on the twenty-ninth of the month [July], at the extremity of a cape [Crown Point, New York] which projects into the lake on the west side, we met the Iroquois on the war-path. Both they and we began to utter loud shouts and each got his arms ready. We drew out into the lake and the Iroquois landed and arranged all their canoes near one another. Then they began to fell trees with the poor axes which they sometimes win in war, or with stone axes; and they barricaded themselves well.

Our Indians all night long also kept their canoes close to one another and tied to poles in order not to get separated, but to fight all together in case of need. We were on the water within bowshot of their barricades. And when they were armed, and everything in order, they sent two canoes which they had separated from the rest, to learn from their enemies whether they wished to fight, and these replied that they had no other desire, but that for the moment nothing could be seen and that it was necessary to wait for daylight in order to distinguish one another. They said that as soon as the sun should rise, they would attack us, and to this our Indians agreed. Meanwhile the whole night was spent in dances and songs on both sides, with many insults and other remarks, such as the lack of courage of our side, how little we could resist or do against them, and that when daylight came our people would learn all this to their ruin. Our side too was not lacking in retort, telling the enemy that they would see such deeds of arms as they had never seen, and a great deal of other talk, such as is usual at the siege of a city. Having sung, danced, and flung words at one another for some time, when daylight came, my companions and I were still hidden, lest the enemy should see us, getting our fire-arms ready as best we could, being however still separated, each in a canoe of the Montagnais Indians. After we were armed with light weapons, we took, each of us, an arquebus[2] and went ashore. I saw the enemy come out of their barricade to the number of two hundred, in appearance strong, robust men. They came slowly to meet us with a gravity and calm which I admired; and at their head were three chiefs. Our Indians likewise advanced in similar order, and told me that those who had the three big plumes were the chiefs, and that there were only these three, whom you could recognize by these plumes, which were larger than those of their companions; and I was to do what I could to kill them. I promised them to do all in my power, and told them that I was very sorry they could not understand me, so that I might direct their method of attacking the enemy, all of whom undoubtedly we should thus defeat; but that there was no help for it, and that I was very glad to show them, as soon as the engagement began, the courage and readiness which were in me.

As soon as we landed, our Indians began to run some two hundred yards towards their enemies, who stood firm and had not yet noticed my white [French] companions who went off into the woods with some Indians. Our Indians began to call to me with loud cries; and to make way for me they divided into two groups, and put me ahead some twenty yards, and I marched on until I was within some thirty yards of the enemy, who as soon as they caught sight of me halted and gazed at me and I at them. When I saw them make a move to draw their bows upon us, I took aim with my arquebus and shot straight at one of the three chiefs, and with this shot two fell to the ground and one of their companions was wounded who died thereof a little later. I had put four bullets into my arquebus. As soon as our people saw this shot so favourable for them, they began to shout so loudly that one could not have heard it thunder, and meanwhile the arrows flew thick on both sides. The Iroquois were much astonished that two men should have been killed so quickly, although they were provided with shields made of cotton thread woven together and wood, which were proof against their arrows. This

---

[2] A muzzle-loaded firearm used in the fifteenth and sixteenth centuries.

frightened them greatly. As I was reloading my arquebus, one of my companions fired a shot from within the woods, which astonished them again so much that, seeing their chiefs dead, they lost courage and took to flight, abandoning the field and their fort, and fleeing into the depth of the forest, whither I pursued them and laid low still more of them. Our Indians also killed several and took ten or twelve prisoners. The remainder fled with the wounded. Of our Indians fifteen or sixteen were wounded with arrows, but these were quickly healed.

After we had gained the victory, our Indians wasted time in taking a large quantity of Indian corn and meal belonging to the enemy, as well as their shields, which they had left behind, the better to run. Having feasted, danced, and sung, we three hours later set off for home with the prisoners. The place where this attack took place is in 43° and some minutes of latitude, and was named Lake Champlain. [See p. 88.]

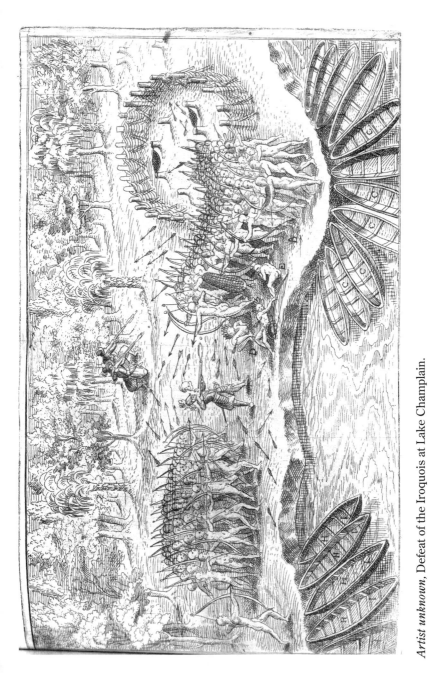

Artist unknown, Defeat of the Iroquois at Lake Champlain.
This image is most likely based on a draft by Champlain's own hand. It also represents the only authentic image of Champlain (center with plumed helmet) that we have.

12

SAMUEL DE CHAMPLAIN

In Huronia — Observations and
a Military Alliance
1615–1616

In October 1615, Champlain and the Huron had attacked an Iroquois
fort just south of Lake Oneida (in what is now upstate New York).
Although the Huron seem to have been satisfied with the outcome of the
battle, since they escaped with captives and demonstrated their cour-
age and ability to raid Iroquois territory, Champlain was disappointed
because he could not persuade them to use European siege warfare
techniques, and the attacks on the Iroquois fort failed as a result. Cham-
plain and the Huron had different ideas regarding military strategy and
the meaning and purpose of waging war, a cultural difference we also
see illustrated in the preceding document when Champlain went to war
against the Iroquois in the company of his Montagnais allies. Cham-
plain was wounded in the knee in this less successful battle and suffered
immensely during the retreat. The Huron obliged him to spend the winter
of 1615–1616 with them, and although he was eager to return to
Québec he made good use of his time in Huronia observing and record-
ing their society. In this excerpt from his Voyages and Discoveries Made
in New France, from the Year 1615 until the End of the Year 1618,
Champlain describes with his characteristic close observation and detail
the Huron people with whom he spent the winter of 1615–1616.

During the winter season, which lasted four months, I had leisure
enough to study their country, their manners, customs, modes of life,
the form of their assemblies, and other things which I should like to
describe. . . .

The region of the Attigouautan tribe [a tribe of the Huron confed-
eracy] lies in latitude 44° 30′, and is two hundred and thirty leagues in

---

Samuel de Champlain, *Voyages and Discoveries Made in New France, from the Year 1615*
to the End of the Year 1618 (1619), vol. 3, trans. H. H. Langton and W. F. Ganong, in *The*
Works of Samuel de Champlain, ed. Henry Percival Biggar et al. (Toronto: Champlain
Society, 1922–1935; Toronto: University of Toronto Press, 1971), 114–55.

length to the west, and ten in breadth, and in this extent of country there are eighteen villages, six of which are enclosed and fortified by wooden palisades in three tiers, interlaced into one another, on top of which they have galleries which they furnish with stones for hurling, and water to extinguish the fire that their enemies might lay against their palisades. This country is fine and pleasant, for the most part cleared, shaped like Brittany and similarly situated, being almost surrounded and enclosed by the Freshwater Sea [Lake Huron]. They calculate that these eighteen villages are peopled by two thousand warriors, without including in this the ordinary inhabitants, who may amount to 30,000 souls. Their lodges are fashioned like bowers or arbours, covered with tree-bark, twenty-five to thirty fathoms long more or less, and six wide, leaving in the middle a passage from ten to twelve feet wide which runs from one end to the other. On both sides is a sort of platform, four feet in height, on which they sleep in summer to escape the annoyance of fleas of which they have many, and in winter they lie beneath on mats near the fire in order to be warmer than on top of the platform. They gather a supply of dry wood and fill their cabins with it, to burn in winter, and at the end of these cabins is a space where they keep their Indian corn, which they put in great casks, made of tree-bark, in the middle of their lodge. Pieces of wood are suspended on which they put their clothes, provisions and other things for fear of mice which are in great numbers. In one such cabin there will be twelve fires, which make twenty-four households, and there is smoke in good earnest, causing many to have great eye troubles, to which they are subject, even towards the end of their lives losing their sight; for there is no window nor opening except in the roof of their cabins by which the smoke can escape. This is all that can be said and known of their ways; for I have described to you completely, as far as they may be known, these dwellings of these people, which is also that of all the tribes that dwell in these parts of the country. They sometimes change their village site after ten, twenty or thirty years, and move it one, two or three leagues from the former spot, if they are not forced by their enemies to decamp and move to a greater distance, as did the Onondagas, some forty to fifty leagues.[1] This is the shape of their

---

[1] Although the Huron were themselves an Iroquoian people, whose dwellings and language resembled those of the Iroquois of present-day New York, they were at war with the Iroquois confederacy, which was based south of Lake Ontario and to which the Onondaga people belonged. Pressure from the Iroquois confederacy was pushing the Huron to relocate northward.

dwellings, which are separated from one another about three to four yards for fear of fire which they greatly dread.

Their life is wretched by comparison with ours, but happy for them since they have not tasted a better and believe that none more excellent can be found. Their principal food and usual sustenance is Indian corn and red beans, which they prepare in several ways. They pound them in wooden mortars and reduce them to flour from which they take the hull by means of certain fans made of tree-bark, and of this flour they make bread with beans which they first boil, as they do Indian corn for soup, because it is easier to beat up, and they mix it all together. Sometimes they put in blueberries or dried raspberries; at other times they put pieces of deer-fat, but not often because it is very scarce with them. Afterwards, steeping the whole in warm water, they make loaves of it, shaped like cakes or tarts, which they bake in the ashes, and when cooked, wash them; and very often they make others out of them, wrapping them in leaves of Indian corn fastened together, and put them into boiling water. But this is not their ordinary kind, for they make another which they call Migan, that is, they take pounded Indian corn without removing the bran, of which they put two or three handfuls into an earthen pot full of water, boil it, stirring it from time to time lest it burn or stick to the pot, then put into the same pot a little fish, fresh or dried according to the season, to give a taste to the said Migan, which is the name they give it. . . .

In [the figure on p. 94] you will see how the women pound their Indian corn. And to prepare it they cook a quantity of fish and meat which they cut up into pieces, then put it into large kettles filled with water, letting it boil well. After this they skim with a spoon the fat which comes from the meat and fish, then add this roasted meal, stirring it constantly until the said Migan is cooked and becomes thick like soup. They give and serve out a portion to each person, with a spoonful of the fat. This they are in the habit of doing at banquets, and not as an ordinary thing, in fact very seldom. Now the said young corn roasted, like that described above, is highly esteemed among them. They also eat beans which they boil with the bulk of the roasted meal, adding to it a little fat and fish. Dogs are in demand at their banquets which they often give each other, especially during the winter when they are at leisure. If they go deer-hunting or fishing they keep what they get for these banquets, having nothing left in their cabins but thin Migan for ordinary use which is like the bran-mash given to pigs. They have another way of eating Indian corn, to prepare which they take it in the ear and put it in water under the mud, leaving it two or three months in that state, until they judge that it is putrid; then they take it out and boil it with meat or fish and then eat it. They also roast it, and it is better that way than boiled, but I assure you that nothing smells so bad as this corn when it comes out of the water all covered with mud; yet the women and children take it and suck it like sugar-cane, there being nothing they like better, as they plainly show. Their usual custom is to have only two meals a day. For ourselves we fasted the whole of Lent, more especially to stir them by an example, but it was time wasted. They also fatten bears, which they keep for two or three years, for their usual feasts. I realised that if these people had cattle, they would be careful of them and would keep them quite well when they had been shown how to feed them, an easy thing for them to do since they have in their country good pastures in abundance for every variety of stock—horses, cows, sheep, pigs and other kinds—for lack of which animals they are thought to be badly off as indeed they appear to be. Nevertheless with all their wretchedness I consider them happy, since they have no other ambition than to live and to support themselves, and they are more secure than those who wander through the forests like brute beasts. They also eat much squash, which they boil and roast in the ashes. As to their clothing they have several kinds and styles, and varieties of wild beasts' skins, both of those they catch and others they exchange for their Indian corn, meal, wampum and fish nets, with the Algonquins, Piserenis [Nipissings], and other tribes who are hunters and have no fixed abodes. All their clothes are of the same make, without variety of new designs. They dress and prepare the skins very well, making their breeches of a moderately large deer-skin, and of another their leggings which reach as high as the waist, with many folds; their moccasins are made of the skins of deer, bear and beaver, of which they use great numbers. Further they have a robe of the same fur, shaped like a cloak, which they wear in the Irish or Egyptian fashion, and sleeves which are tied behind by a cord. That is how they are dressed during the winter. . . . When they go into the fields they gird their robe about their body, but when in their village they leave off their sleeves and do not gird themselves. The Milan trimmings to adorn their clothing are made of glue and of the scrapings of the said skins, with which they make bands in many ways, as they fancy, in places putting bands of red or brown paint amidst those of the glue which are always pale, and do not lose their markings however dirty they may get. Among these tribes are some more skilful than others in preparing skins and clever in inventing patterns to put upon their clothes. Above all others our Montagnais and Algonquins are those that take most trouble with it; for they put on their robes strips of porcupine-quill which they dye a very beautiful scarlet colour; they value these strips very highly and take them off to make them serve for other robes when they wish to make a change. They also use them to beautify the face and have a better appearance when they wish to deck themselves out. Most of them paint their faces black and red, mixing the paint with oil made from the seed of the sunflower or else with bear fat or that of other animals, and they also dye their hair, which some wear long, others short, others on one side only. As to the women and girls, they wear it always in the same manner; they are clad like the men except that they always gird up their robes, which hang down to the knee. In this they differ from the men; they are not ashamed to show their body, that is, from the waist up and from mid-thigh down, always keeping the rest covered, and they are laden with quantities of wampum, both necklaces and chains, which they allow to hang in front of their robes and attached to their belts, and also with bracelets and ear-rings. They have their hair well combed, dyed and oiled, and thus they go to the dances with a tuft of their hair behind tied up with eel-skin which they arrange to serve as a band, or sometimes they fasten to it plates a foot square covered with the same wampum, which hang behind. In this manner, gaily dressed and adorned, they like to show themselves at dances, where their fathers and mothers send them, forgetting no device that they can apply to bedeck and bedizen their daughters; and I can assure you that at dances I have attended, I have seen girls that had more than twelve pounds of wampum on them, without counting the other trifles with which they are loaded and decked out. On this page may be seen how the women are dressed, as is shown in F, and the girls going to the dance in G [see p. 94].

All these people are of a very cheerful disposition although many among them are of a sad and saturnine humour. They are well-proportioned in body; the men being well shaped, strong and robust, as also the women and girls, a good number of whom are pleasing and pretty both in figure, complexion and features, all in harmony. Their breasts hang down very little except when they are old. Among these tribes are found powerful women of extraordinary stature; for it is they who have almost the whole care of the house and the work; for they till the soil, sow the Indian corn, fetch wood for the winter, strip the hemp and spin it, and with the thread make fishing-nets for catching fish, and other necessary things they have to do: likewise they have the labour of harvesting the corn, storing it, preparing food, and attending to the house, and besides are required to follow and accompany their husbands from

Artist unknown, Native costumes, based on Champlain's description in the text.

place to place, in the fields, where they serve as mules to carry the baggage, with a thousand other kinds of duties and services that the women fulfil and are required to carry out. As to the men, they do nothing but hunt deer and other animals, fish, build lodges and go on the war-path.

Having done this, they visit other tribes, where they have access and acquaintance, to trade and exchange what they have for what they have not, and on their return do not cease from feasting and dancing, with which they entertain one another, and afterwards they go to sleep, which is their finest exertion.[2] . . .

As for their laws I did not see that they have any, nor anything approaching them; as indeed is the case, inasmuch as there is with them no correction, punishment or censure of evil-doers except by way of revenge, rendering evil for evil, not as a matter of law but through passion, engendering wars and quarrels which exist amongst them most of the time.

Moreover, they recognise no divinity, they adore and believe in no God nor in anything whatsoever, but live like brute beasts. They have indeed some regard for the Devil, or a similar name, although this is a matter of doubt because in the word they use are included different meanings and it embraces in itself several things: so that it cannot easily be known and determined whether they mean the Devil or something else, but what makes one rather believe that it is the Devil whom they mean, is that when they see a man doing something extraordinary, or cleverer than usual, or indeed a valiant warrior, or else infuriated as if out of his mind and beside himself, they call him Oqui [a person possessed by a powerful spirit], as we should say, a great well-informed mind or a great Devil. However this may be, they have certain persons who act as Oquis or Manitous, as the Algonquins and Montagnais call them, and this sort of folk are doctors, to heal the sick and bind up the wounded, to predict future events, in short [to practise] all abuses and delusions of the Devil in order to mislead and deceive them. These Oquis or seers persuade their patients and the sick to make and have held feasts and

[2] Europeans found the division of labor in Native societies in both Africa and the New World unsettling because in Europe only male nobles avoided agricultural or artisan labor and devoted themselves instead to hunting and war. In other societies, such as those described here, agriculture was an outgrowth of gathering, and both types of labor, as well as making clothing, were considered women's work, whereas hunting, diplomacy and politics, and war were the domain of men. This led to frequent misunderstandings when Europeans encountered societies with this type of gendered division of labor because the Europeans tended to assume that the men in these societies were simply lazy compared to European male peasants who farmed and wove cloth and in fact traditionally were prohibited from engaging in hunting or carrying a sword.

certain ceremonies in order to be the sooner cured, their intent being to take part in them and gain the greatest possible advantage for themselves and, by the hope of a speedier cure, they get them to hold many other ceremonies which I shall describe farther on in the proper place. These are the people in whom they place most belief, but to be possessed by the Devil and tormented, like other savages farther off than they, is what is seen very rarely. This affords more opportunity and reason for believing that to bring them to the knowledge of God would be easier if their country were inhabited by persons who would take the trouble and the task of teaching them. It is not sufficient to send friars there, if there are no persons to support and assist them: for though these people are desirous to-day of knowing what God is, to-morrow this desire will change when it becomes necessary to do away with and put an end to their filthy habits, the looseness of their morals and their rude licence. Thus inhabitants and families are needed to keep them to their duty and by gentle treatment to constrain them to do better and by good example to incite them to correct living. Father Joseph[3] and I have many times conversed with them on our belief, laws and customs; they listened attentively in their councils, saying to us sometimes, "You say things that pass our understanding and that we cannot comprehend by words, as something beyond our intelligence; but if you would do well [by us], you should dwell in our country and bring women and children, and when they come to these regions we shall see how you serve this God whom you worship, and your mode of life with your wives and children, your way of tilling the ground and sowing, and how you obey your laws and your manner of feeding animals, and how you manufacture all that we see proceeding from your invention. Seeing this we shall learn more in one year than hearing your discourses in twenty, and if we cannot understand, you shall take our children who will be like your own: and thus judging our life wretched by comparison with yours, it is easy to believe that we shall adopt yours and abandon our own." Their speech seemed to me natural good sense, showing their desire to know God. . . .

As for the sick, a man or woman struck down or affected by some disease sends for the Oqui, who on arrival visits the sick person and learns and informs himself of his disease and pain. After that, the said Oqui sends for a great number of men, women and girls, with three or four old women, just as the said Oqui orders, and these enter the cabin dancing,

[3] Father Joseph was one of the Récollet priests working with the Natives in New France. Because Champlain supported bringing the Récollet missionaries to New France, he conferred with them frequently and relied on their advice, as he was later to do with the Jesuits in New France as well.

each with a bearskin or the skin of some other beast over her head, but a bearskin is the commonest since nothing is more frightful, and there will be two or three other old women near the sick person or patient, who most frequently is feigning or imagining sickness. But of this sickness they are soon cured, and they most frequently hold feasts at the expense of their friends or relatives who give them something to put into the kettle, besides those things they receive as presents from the dancers, male and female, such as wampum and other trifles, so that they are soon cured; for when they see that nothing more is to be expected they get up, with what they have been able to accumulate. But others really sick are not readily cured by such playing and dancing and goings on. To return to my narrative, the old women who are near the sick person receive the presents, each singing in turn, and then stopping; and when all the presents are made, they begin to lift up their voices with one accord, singing all together, and beating time with sticks on dry tree-bark; whereupon all the women and girls begin to place themselves at the extremity of the cabin as if for the purpose of making their entry in a ballet or masquerade, the old women walking in front with bearskins over their heads and all the rest following them one after another. They have only two kinds of dances with some sort of measure, one of four steps and the other of twelve, like the *trioly* of Brittany. They dance very gracefully, the young men often joining in. Having danced for an hour or two, the old women take hold of the sick woman to make her dance, and she pretends to get up sadly, then begins to dance, and once at it, after some space of time, she will dance and enjoy herself as much as the others. You can imagine how sick she must be. Below is the representation of their dances [see the figure on p. 98].

The medicine-man thereby gains honour and reputation, at the sight of his patient being so soon cured and on his feet; which does not happen to those who are in extremities and overcome with weakness; for this kind of medicine gives them death rather than healing; for I assure you that sometimes they make such a noise and din, from morning till two o'clock at night, that it is impossible for the patient to bear it except with great difficulty. Sometimes a fancy will seize the patient to make the women and girls dance all together, but it must be by order of the Oqui, and this is not all, for he and the Manitou, accompanied by some others, will make grimaces and incantations and contortions to such an extent that they generally become as it were beside themselves, like lunatics and madmen, throwing fire about the cabin from one side to the other, swallowing red-hot coals, holding them for a time in their hands, also throwing red-hot cinders into the eyes of the other onlookers; and, on

Artist unknown, Hurons dancing in religious ceremony, based on Champlain's description in the text.

seeing them in this state, one would say that the Devil, Oqui, or Manitou, if such we must call him, possesses them and torments them in that manner. And when this noise and din is over, they withdraw each to his own quarters. . . . However, it sometimes happens that three or four of these sick persons get well, rather by happy accident and chance than by science, which only confirms their false belief, so that they are persuaded they have been cured by means of these ceremonies, not bearing in mind that for two who get cured ten others die from the noise and great din and the blowings they make, which is more fitted to kill than to cure a sick person; but that they should expect to recover their health by this noise and we on the contrary by quiet and rest, shows how the devil does everything the wrong way about. There are also women who go into these rages, but they do not do so much harm; they walk on all fours like beasts. Seeing this the magician called the Oqui begins to sing, then with some grimaces blows upon her, ordering her to drink certain waters and immediately to give a feast either of fish or of flesh, which must be found, even if it be scarce at the time; nevertheless this is done at once. When the shouting is over and the banquet finished, they return each to his cabin until the next time he comes to pay her a visit, blowing upon her and singing, with several others summoned for that purpose, holding in their hands a dry tortoise-shell filled with little pebbles which they rattle in the ears of the sick woman, ordering her to make forthwith three or four feasts, and a singing and dancing party, at which all the girls appear decked out and painted, as I have represented in figure G [p. 94]. . . . The said Oqui will order masquerades and disguises like those who run about the streets on Mardi-Gras in France. Thus they go and sing near the sick woman's couch, and parade the length of the village while the feast is being prepared for the masquers, who return very tired, having taken enough exercise to empty the kettle of its Migan.

4

Administrator and Diplomat

13

SAMUEL DE CHAMPLAIN

Two Ceremonies in Acadia: A Souriquois Funeral and the Order of Good Cheer
1606–1607

Champlain spent the winter of 1606–1607 at Port-Royal in Acadia, in the company of Jean de Biencourt, Sieur de Poutrincourt, leader of the Port-Royal settlement, and Marc Lescarbot. Champlain had become convinced that one reason for the high mortality among the French during previous winters, besides the harsh climate of New France, had been poor morale and a lack of fresh food. During the winter of 1606–1607, Champlain resolved therefore to remedy both of these problems through the creation of his Order of Good Cheer. Modeled on the traditional military/religious orders of medieval France, each member of the Order (the more prominent members of the little settlement at Port-Royal) would take a turn wearing a ceremonial medal and taking charge of procuring food for a feast that evening. The member in charge each day acted as a sort of master of ceremonies and was responsible for organizing hunting parties to provision the table with fresh meat, overseeing the preparation of the food, and presiding over entertainment during the meal—songs, poetry, speeches. After the feast, the medal and responsibilities would rotate with a small ceremony to the next in line in the Order. The more prominent

Samuel de Champlain, *The Voyages of the Sieur de Champlain of Saintonge, Captain in the Ordinary for the King in the Navy* (1613), vol. 1, trans. H. H. Langton and W. F. Ganong, in *The Works of Samuel de Champlain*, ed. Henry Percival Biggar et al. (Toronto: Champlain Society, 1922–1935; Toronto: University of Toronto Press, 1971), 438–51.

Acadian Natives present at Port-Royal would be welcomed to join the feast as well.

Champlain also had the opportunity to observe a funeral ceremony of the Native Souriquois people during the winter. A Souriquois (Mi'kmaq) named Panonias had been killed as a result of a quarrel between some Souriquois and Natives of Norumbega (present-day Maine). The Souriquois sagamore Membertou, a steadfast ally of the French, presided over the ceremony, which Champlain describes in great detail here, giving us the best description of Mi'kmaq funeral customs we possess.

Upon our arrival, Lescarbot, who had remained at the settlement, along with the others who had stayed there, welcomed us with sundry jollities for our entertainment.

Having landed, and recovered breath, each began to make small gardens, and I myself began to take care of mine, in preparation for the spring, in order to sow several kinds of seed which we had brought from France and which throve extremely well in all the gardens.

The Sieur de Poutrincourt on the other hand had a water-mill built about a league and a half from our settlement, close to the point where wheat had been sown. The mill was built near a waterfall formed by a small river which is not navigable on account of the number of rocks in it, and which falls into a small lake. At this place is such abundance of herring in their season that one could fill shallops with them, if one would take the trouble and bring thither the requisite appliances. Indeed the Indians of these parts come there at times to fish. Here we also made a quantity of charcoal for our forge. During the winter, in order not to be idle, I undertook to construct a road along the edge of the woods leading to a little river, which is like a brook, and which we named the troutery, for the reason that there were in it many of these fish. I asked the Sieur de Poutrincourt for two or three men, whom he gave me to assist me in making this walk. I got on so well that in a short time I had cleared it. It extends as far as the troutery, and is nearly two thousand paces long; and served as our promenade under the shade of the trees I had left standing on both sides. This induced the Sieur de Poutrincourt to have another made through the woods as a direct route to the entrance of Port Royal, about three and a half leagues by land from our settlement. He had a beginning made from the troutery for about half a league, but never finished it because the labour was too great, and he was busy with other things then more necessary.

Some time after our arrival, we caught sight of a shallop in which were some Indians, who informed us that at the place whence they came, which was Norumbega, an Indian, who was one of our friends, had been killed out of vengeance because another Indian, Iouaniscou, and his people had killed some Indians from Norumbega and Kennebec, as I have already related; and that the Etechemins had told this to Secoudon, the Indian who was at that time with us.

The Indian in command of the boat was called Ouagimou, who was on familiar terms with Bessabes, chief of Norumbega river, from whom he asked the body of Panonias who had been killed. Bessabes granted him this, begging him to say to his friends that he was very sorry for Panonias' death, assuring Ouagimou that it was without his knowledge that Panonias had been killed, and that, since it was not his fault, he begged him to say to them that he hoped they would remain friends as heretofore. This Ouagimou promised to do on his return home. He told us he was much worried until he got away from them, however much friendliness they showed him; for they were liable to change, and he feared lest they would treat him as they had him who was slain. Accordingly he did not tarry long after his dismissal. He brought the body in his shallop from Norumbega to our settlement, a distance of fifty leagues.

As soon as the body was brought on shore, the relatives and friends began to make outcries beside it, their faces being painted all over with black, which is their manner of mourning. After a great deal of weeping, they took a quantity of tobacco and two or three dogs and other things belonging to the deceased, and burnt them upon the shore some thousand paces from our settlement. Their cries continued until they had returned to their wigwams.

The next day they took the body and wrapped it in a red coverlet which Membertou, the chief of these parts, had much importuned me to give him, inasmuch as it was handsome and large. This he presented to the relatives of the dead man, who thanked me very much for it. Then after having bound up the body, they decorated it with many kinds of ornaments, such as beads and bracelets of several colours; painted his face, and upon his head stuck many feathers and other objects the fairest they had. Then they placed the body on its knees between two stakes, with another supporting it under the arms; and about the body were his mother, his wife, and other relatives and friends, both women and girls, who howled like dogs.

Whilst the women and girls were lamenting, the Indian named Membertou made a speech to his companions upon the death of the deceased, inciting each to take vengeance for the wickedness and treachery committed by the subjects of Bessabes, and to make war on them as soon as possible. All promised him to do so in the spring.

When the speech was finished and the cries over, they carried the body of the dead man into another wigwam. Having smoked, they again wrapped it in a moose-skin and tied it up very securely, and preserved it until there should be a larger number of Indians present, from each of whom the brother of the dead man expected to receive presents, since it is their custom to give such to those who have lost their fathers, mothers, wives, brothers, or sisters.

On the night of the twenty-sixth of December, a wind from the southeast blew down a number of trees.

The last day of December it began to snow, and continued to do so until the next morning.

On the sixteenth of January following, in the year 1607, the Sieur de Poutrincourt, wishing to go to the head of Equille river, found it closed with ice some two leagues from our settlement, and had to return since he was unable to go farther.

On the eighth of February some ice-floes began to come down from the head of the river into the port, which only freezes along the shore.

On the tenth of May following it snowed the whole night, and towards the end of the month there were several heavy white frosts which lasted as late as the tenth and twelfth of June, when all the trees were covered with leaves, except the oaks which do not put out theirs until about the fifteenth.

The winter was not so long as in the preceding years, nor did the snow remain so late upon the ground. It rained pretty often, on which account the Indians suffered a severe famine because of the scarcity of snow.[1] The Sieur de Poutrincourt fed part of those who were with us, that is to say Membertou[,] his wife and his children, and some others.

We spent this winter very pleasantly, and had good fare by means of the Order of Good Cheer which I established, and which everybody found beneficial to his health, and more profitable than all sorts of medicine we might have used. This Order consisted of a chain which we used to place with certain little ceremonies about the neck of one of our people, commissioning him for that day to go hunting. The next day it was conferred upon another, and so on in order. All vied with each other to see who could do the best, and bring back the finest game. We did not come off badly, nor did the Indians who were with us.

---

[1] Heavy snow actually aided hunting, especially of moose, which were more easily run down in deep drifts.

There was scurvy among our men, but not so violent as it had been in the previous years. Nevertheless, seven of them died, as did another from an arrow-shot received from the Indians at Misfortune harbour.

Our surgeon, named Master Stephen, opened a few bodies, and, as had been done in the other cases in the previous years, found almost all the interior parts affected. Some eight or ten who were sick got well in the spring.

At the beginning of March and of April, each began to prepare the gardens for the sowing of the seeds in May, which is the proper season. These seeds came up just as well as they could have done in France, but a little later. I believe that in France the season is at the most a month and a half earlier. As I have said, the season for sowing is in May, although sometimes one can sow in April; but such sowings advance no faster than those made in May, when there are no longer any frosts that can injure the plants except the very tender ones; for there are many that cannot withstand the white frosts except after much care and labour.

On the twenty-fourth of May we caught sight of a small pinnace of six to seven tons' burden, which we sent men to examine. They found it was a young man of St. Malo, named Chevalier, who brought letters from the Sieur de Monts to the Sieur de Poutrincourt, by which he directed the latter to bring back his company to France.[2] He told us of the birth of Monseigneur the Duke of Orleans, which rejoiced us, and in honour thereof we made bonfires and chanted the *Te Deum*.

---

[2] De Mons had ordered the return of the colony to France because his enemies had persuaded Henri IV to revoke de Mons's monopoly on the fur trade. On the brink of bankruptcy, de Mons had to dissolve the company.

14

SAMUEL DE CHAMPLAIN

On Mediating Struggles over the Fur Trade
1620

After a relatively uneventful winter, in May 1621 the arrival of a ship from France created a situation that put Champlain's administrative and diplomatic skills to the test once again. As this excerpt from Champlain's The Voyages of the Sieur de Champlain *(1632) recounts, the new viceroy, the duke of Montmorency (1595–1632), had worked out a settlement with the new holders of the fur trade monopoly, the Protestant merchant Guillaume de Caën and his uncle Ezéchiel de Caën and cousin Émery de Caën. This altered state of affairs sparked rising tensions in the settlement as merchants from the old fur trading company had already sent ships to engage in the fur trade for that year. The head of their fleet was none other than Champlain's old friend François Gravé, Sieur du Pont, which made the situation even more delicate for Champlain. Given the large investment the shareholders of the old company had made in equipping and sending out a fleet, Pont-Gravé was determined to trade anyway, whereas Guillaume de Caën was equally determined to prevent him and to confiscate Pont-Gravé's ship and merchandise in order to demonstrate the primacy of the new monopoly company. Champlain was caught in the middle of this conflict, which threatened to become violent as members of the colony began to take sides. While explaining this crisis and his course of action, Champlain also discusses the frustrations he experienced dealing with the unruly settlers and fur traders of New France and his own views on how, ideally, the colony should be administered.*

Samuel de Champlain, *The Voyages of the Sieur de Champlain, Second Part* (1632), vol. 5, bk. 1, trans. W. D. Lesueur, in *The Works of Samuel de Champlain*, ed. Henry Percival Biggar et al. (Toronto: Champlain Society, 1922–1935; Toronto: University of Toronto Press, 1971), 11–31.

On the fifteenth of May [1621] a pinnace [small boat] being ready, it was put into the water and laden with provisions for trading with the savages at Tadoussac. Le Mons, the chief clerk, embarked in it with seven others, and on the way fell in with a shallop on board of which were Captain du May and Guers, Commissioners of my Lord de Montmorency, with five sailors, three soldiers, and a boy. Our clerk consequently turned back, and they all came back together to our settlement. . . .

The said Guers handed me letters which it had pleased the King and my Lord to do me the honour of writing to me, together with one from Monsieur de Puisieux, and others from the Sieurs Dolu, de Villemenon, and de Caen. The King's was as follows:

> Champlain, I have seen by your letters of the fifteenth of August with what earnestness you are working over there at your settlement, and for the good of my service; and not only do I feel very thankful to you for this, but it will give me pleasure to recognize it to your advantage when opportunity offers. Meantime I have very readily granted some munitions of war for which application was made to me, in order to increase your means of subsistence, and enable you to continue in this good line of duty, which, knowing your care and fidelity, I fully count upon your doing. At Paris, the twenty-fourth day of February, 1621, signed, Louis, and underneath, Brulart.

Following that of his Majesty I received another letter from Monsieur de Puisieux, Secretary of State, in which he told me, amongst other things, that the Sieur Dolu had asked for arms to send to me, and that the request had been granted and the arms forwarded. Previously my Lord the Duke of Montmorency wrote to me as follows:

> Mr. Champlain. For several reasons I have thought it right to exclude the old shareholders from Rouen and St. Malo in the trade to New France from returning to that country. And, to render you assistance and provide you with what is necessary, I have chosen the Sieurs de Caen, uncle and nephew, and their associates; the first is a good merchant and the second a good sea-captain, so that he will be able to help you effectually and cause the authority of the King to be recognized in those distant regions under my government. I recommend you to assist him and those who shall go out with his authority, against all others, in order to maintain them in the enjoyment of the privileges which I have granted to them. I have instructed the Sieur Dolu, Intendant of the affairs of the country, to send you a copy of the contract by the first vessel, in order that you may know what they are under obligation to do, and hold them to the execution thereof; as I on my part desire to fulfil all I have promised to them. I have taken care to provide for the

continued payment of your salary, since I believe you will desire to go on rendering good service to the King; as also, in good will to yourself, I remain, Mr. Champlain, your most affectionate and perfect friend, signed, MONTMORENCY. From Paris, the second of February, 1621.

The letters of the Sieur Dolu instructed me to stop the operations of the clerks [heretofore in charge], and to take possession of all the goods, both those obtained by trade and those intended to be used in trade, on account of the claims which the King and his said Lordship advanced against the said former Company, on the ground of their not having discharged their obligations in the matter of colonization. As to the Sieur de Caen, although he was of the opposite religion, there were great hopes of his becoming a Catholic; and, as to the exercise of his religion, I was to tell him that he was not to practise it either on land or on sea; and as to anything further I was to use my own judgment. The letter of the Sieur de Villemenon, Intendant of the Admiralty, was of much the same tenour: that of the said Sieur de Caen, which was to the same effect, mentioned that he was coming out with two good ships well armed and with ample stores of all things necessary both for himself and for our settlement, and that he hoped to bring with him some good official declarations in his favour. Moreover, having summoned the Sieur du May and Guers, the commissioner, and also Father Georges, to whom my Lord and the Sieurs Dolu and Villemenon had written letters to the same purport as those to myself, enjoining me not to do anything without communicating it to him, I determined that no loss of any kind should occur, and that it was necessary to make no change before the arrival of the said Sieur de Caen, who had all proper authority, bearing with him a decree in his favour, authorizing him to seize both ships and merchandise; and that meantime I should keep all the furs until it could be seen on what grounds they could be justly taken and seized.

Moreover I had to consider the difficulties which the other parties might make, as I held no power from the King, and as the said clerk would not submit to any lesser authority, certainly not to such advices as we had received from France. The said clerk was informed of the situation by the sailors of the Sieur du May, who started a rumour that the said Sieur de Caen would seize all that belonged to the former Company as soon as he arrived; and they so worked upon the mind of the clerk and all his people that they determined among themselves not to permit any seizure of their goods until I could produce a letter or order from the King, which I was not able to do; while all those who depended on the shareholders, including their hired men, fearing to lose their wages, as they were told they would do, took the position that, as they were the stronger party, they would prevent a seizure if they could, should I be disposed to attempt one. That is why, in a country like this, while a company holds the purse-strings, it pays, gives, and assists according to its own good pleasure; but those who command in his Majesty's name get scant obedience, having no one to assist them save those subject to the good pleasure of the Company, who have nothing they are so opposed to as those who are placed in authority by the King or the Viceroys, for the reason that these are not dependent on them. They do not want anyone to observe or judge what they do or their proceedings or methods of business, their one object being to get everything for themselves. Let them only make their profit, they care little what happens. As to forts, great or small, they do not want them until some necessity arises, and then it is too late. When I talked to them about fortifying, they were annoyed; in vain I pointed out to them the disadvantages that might arise from the lack of them, they were deaf; and the whole reason of that was their fear lest, if there were a fort, they should be mastered and brought under the law. And while they were harbouring these ideas, they were leaving the country and us a prey to any pirate or enemy who, counting on gathering plunder from people who were in a defenceless condition, might pillage everything. I wrote often enough to the members of the Council that orders to this effect should be given, but they never came. . . .

To return to my narrative, the said clerk and all the rest of them began to murmur, saying that the intention was to deprive them of their salaries, and that they might as well surrender their lives as be treated in that fashion. This gave the clerk a pretext for speaking to me again on the subject, and putting forward his side of the case. If I had any order from the King, I need only produce it, he said, to satisfy him and keep everything peaceful. I told him that no harm was going to be done to him or his goods, and that he might go on trading with as much confidence as in the past. This quieted him and everybody else. I reprimanded the Sieur du May's sailors, who had caused all this apprehension by the reports they had spread, and said further that they might rest assured that I was not going to make any changes until the said Sieur de Caen should arrive with a royal decree, which would put everything in order, and would have to be obeyed.

The question was also discussed whether permission to trade should be granted to the Sieur du May, who had brought over goods to be exchanged with the savages for beaver skins; and it was decided that, to avoid all cause of offence, such permission should not be granted; moreover, that they [du May and his men] had no power to do so. When the vessels left France the two Companies were engaged in litigation before his Majesty's Council; the old Company therefore, it was held, could still enjoy the privileges granted to it by the King, subject to the authority of my Lord the Prince, until otherwise ordered. Should, however, the members of the Council give an order so much in favour of the New Company as to confiscate for its benefit [the property of the old], there would be no advantage in his [du May's] trading in the meantime, because everything would be there for him, as he was promising himself; and if, on the other hand, he simply had permission to trade on the same footing as the old Company, we could see the bill of the goods that had been sent out, and he could receive skins to the same value, according to prevailing prices, out of the Company's stores. His vessel would thus lose nothing that it was entitled to, owing to not having traded before receipt of the Council's judgment, which the said Sieur de Caen was to bring with him. Such was the decision arrived at in presence of the Sieur du May and Guers acting on behalf of the new Company.

This having been settled, I dispatch Captain du May on the twenty-fifth of May, to give full information to the Sieur de Caen as to what had taken place and as to the condition in which he had left us, and also to request him to send me additional men.

On the third of June the said du May arrived in a shallop [a two-masted armed vessel] with ten others and advised me of the arrival of the Sieur du Pont in a vessel of a hundred and fifty tons, named the *Salamander*, with a crew of sixty-five, accompanied by all the clerks of the old Company; he enquired at the same time in what capacity I wished to employ him. The news greatly rejoiced the employees of the old Company and all the men who were dependent upon them. It was a reinforcement for them, and had we angered them by a seizure of their goods without some absolute authority from the King or my Lord, they might have done us no small harm; for the small vessel of du May, which was at Tadoussac, the crew of which only numbered eighteen men, might have been seized, and I had only twelve with me at Quebec; and their provisions also were low, which was why I came to the assistance of the said du May.

Having heard the news, I decided to place the said du May in a little fort, already begun, against the wishes of the said clerk, together with my brother-in-law Boullé and eight men, four given to me by the Récollet Fathers out of theirs, and four belonging to the old Company. I had provisions, arms, powder, lead, and other necessary things carried into the place as expeditiously as possible, so as to render it defensible: in this way we could hold our own in negotiation, and meantime continue to work at the fort to strengthen its defences.

For my own part, I remained in the factory [settlement and trading post] with three men of the said du May and four others, servants of the Récollet Fathers, Guers the commissioner, and the remaining men of the factory. The fort made everything safe, with the instructions I had given to the said Captain du May.

On Monday the seventh of the month [June 1621], arrived the pinnace belonging to our factory, in which were the clerks of the old shareholders to the number of three, whereupon I gave instructions to take up arms, assigning to each man his post, and the same was done at the fort; I also raised the drawbridge of the factory. Father Georges, accompanied by Guers, went to the river bank awaiting the landing of the said clerks, desirous of knowing with what instructions they came, and what commission they had, being aware from the advices we had received, of what was going on in France. The clerks reported that they had no order except from their Company, as they still had their rights under the contract and stipulations that I had granted to them under the good pleasure of my Lord the Prince, while awaiting a judgment of the Lords of the Council, which they hoped would be in their favour and against the new Company, which was endeavouring to have their [the old] Company dissolved before the expiration of their term. They added that they had entered a protest against the action of the Admiralty officers who had refused them their sailing-papers, and that, seeing the danger in which their whole business would be placed, in regard both to the men who were here and to the unjust claim made upon their goods, they had determined to fall back on simple obedience to the King.

They said all they wanted to say, and entered into a number of other matters, manifesting great vexation at seeing themselves received in so extraordinary a fashion and one so different from what they had been accustomed to.

The said Father having heard part of their grievances, asked them if they were bringing out any provisions for our support. They said "Yes," and that they felt certain that they were in agreement with his said Lordship, or that they would have a decision in their favour. When they had finished talking, the said Father told them that he was going to report to me and see what I was disposed to do. He accordingly reported to me what they had said, whereupon we took counsel as to what was best to be done.

It was decided, seeing that the said Sieur de Caen had not yet arrived, to adhere to our first resolution in the matter in order to avoid the dangers which might ensue.

It was further decided to admit as many as five clerks, and to let them have their goods, so that they might trade in the upper part of the river St. Lawrence, and to assist them in what they should have to do; to which they assented.

They came into the factory, and there I impressed particularly upon them the will and purpose of his Majesty, pointing out what they had done contrary thereto. The King's commands to me were to maintain the country in peace, and under his obedience; to the same effect were the instructions of my Lord [Montmorency] who had excluded them from the Company by forming a new one. They should not have come out without having in their possession a valid decree from my lords of the Council. However, while awaiting the arrival of the other vessels, which would bring full orders, we would, in a short time, hand over to them a quantity of goods for trade. They accepted this arrangement, and, since we did not desire to be very strict with them, we gave them these goods. They requested to be furnished with arms: these I was obliged to refuse, telling them that they should not have come unprovided. They loaded two pinnaces, and then asked me for the beaver skins that were in the factory. These also I refused to let them have, saying that those skins must not leave the factory as long as we had not provisions enough for maintaining the authority of the King, in case any accident happened to the Sieur de Caen; but that, having these peltries, we could get provisions from the vessels that would bring them to us from Gaspé [in Acadia]. They did all they could to get them, threatening to enter protest against my action in refusing them their peltries and munitions; they also insisted that I should send the said Captain du May and his men out of the fort and the factory, in which I had placed them without instructions from the King. I told them that his Majesty's command to me was to hold the country, and safeguard the place, and that the order of my Lord, which was that of the King, was quite sufficient: that order I was obeying, and I had taken Captain du May into the fort because I had perfect confidence in him. That would be quite right, they said, if he had brought with him a decree of the Council, which he had not done; meanwhile I was determined to maintain my position to the best of my ability, and they should make whatever protests they might wish for their own defence.

When it came to the framing of their protests, I was able to silence them by pointing out to them that they really did not know in what form to do it. The result was that they changed their minds, as they dreaded to commit themselves in a matter which might turn to their disadvantage. And so they embarked for Three Rivers to do their trading, the date being the ninth of June.

15

SAMUEL DE CHAMPLAIN

Conflict and Negotiations with the Natives
1627

In this excerpt from The Voyages of the Sieur de Champlain *(1632), we find Champlain contending with one of the thorniest diplomatic and administrative problems of his career, a young Montagnais warrior's ambush and murder of two Frenchmen. It was clear to Champlain that a Montagnais had committed the crime, even though at first the Montagnais attempted to blame the deaths on marauding Iroquois. Champlain had to find a way to confront the Montagnais in order to satisfy the demands for justice from the settlers and to ensure that the Montagnais did not decide that the French were so weak that they could be attacked with impunity. Yet at the same time he could not afford to anger his Montagnais allies, whose support was crucial to the survival of the colony and the functioning of the fur trade.*

The two peoples' conceptions of justice differed greatly, however, with Europeans focused on individual guilt and public punishment and Natives believing in collective guilt and punishment (hence, their peace offering of three young girls to raise as Catholics in a French household). Champlain found it very difficult to mediate between these opposing cultural systems.

On the third of October [1627], I left Quebec to go to Cape Tourmente to see what progress our workmen had made, and to bring some of them back. Two men returned by land, in order to drive some cattle that were being brought from Cape Tourmente to Quebec. After having settled matters at this place, I returned on the sixth of the month, and on my arrival heard that some savages had murdered these two men in charge of the cattle, as they lay asleep about half a league from our settlement. This distressed me greatly. We went to get the bodies, which

Samuel de Champlain, *The Second Part of the Voyages of the Sieur de Champlain* (1632), vol. 5, bk. 2, trans. W. D. Lesueur, in *The Works of Samuel de Champlain*, ed. Henry Percival Biggar et al. (Toronto: Champlain Society, 1922–1935; Toronto: University of Toronto Press, 1971), 240–51.

had been dragged into the river in order that they might be carried away by the tide. When brought in, they were examined; their skulls had been smashed by blows with axes and there were many other body wounds made by swords and knives.

We concluded that it was advisable to handle this business cautiously, and to discover the murderers as soon as possible in order to punish them, and to see how we should proceed to deal with those ruffians, who have no justice among them. As to taking vengeance upon a number who were not guilty, there would be no sense in that. It would be to declare open war and to ruin the country for a time, until the whole race had been exterminated; and at the same time to destroy our trade, or at least impair it greatly. We were besides in a miserable condition ourselves through lack of munitions of war; and we had to take into account many other disadvantages which might arise if we did things too precipitately. We finally decided to bring together all the captains of the savages, relate the facts, and show them the maltreated bodies of the dead men. This decision we now carried out.

The next day all the chiefs came to our settlement, where we did not spare words in pointing out to them the benefit they received year by year from us; while, contrary to all right and reason, they committed abominable and detestable acts—acts of murder and treachery—and that, if we had the same diabolical spirit that they had, we would, in revenge for the murder of these two men, kill fifty of their people and exterminate them all. [We reminded them] that we had already pardoned them for the murder of two other men; but for this crime we wanted to have the murderers in order to execute justice on them. They were therefore to tell us who were the culprits and hand them over to us, if they wished to live in peace with us. We made it clear that our only resentment was against those that had murdered our men, whose bodies we placed before them.

At first they tried to make out that it was some of the Iroquois that had done the deed, but as there was not the slightest probability of this, we maintained the contrary, that the murder was only the work of their people. Finally they acknowledged that we were right, but said that they did not know which of them had done the deed.

Our people suspected, amongst others, a certain savage, whose name we mentioned, asking them to produce him; which they promised to do. The next day they brought him, and he was questioned about some threatening words he had spoken to some of our men. He denied this and said he had never dreamt of anything so exceedingly wicked as to want to kill Frenchmen, whom he loved as he did himself. Moreover, he had a wife and several children who would have prevented him from committing this murder, even had he been intending to do it. I had them tell him that the murderer in the former case had certainly a wife and children, and that none the less he murdered two of our men, and this notwithstanding the fact that we cherished him more than any other savage of his time; consequently the excuses he was making could not be held sufficient to relieve him of the suspicion he was under. To continue our story: after many things had been said on both sides, we determined to arrest this man pending the handing over to us of three youths belonging to the principal men amongst them, one from the Montagnais, the second from Three Rivers, and the third the son of the suspect himself, [to be held] until they should have delivered to us the man who had committed the crime. They asked for a delay of three days, both that they might deliberate on the matter, and that they might try to discover the murderer; and this we granted.

They went back to their wigwams, and then we had to keep on our guard, both at the fort and at the settlement, giving notice to the Jesuit Fathers and to the men at Cape Tourmente, that every man was to keep careful watch, and not to allow any savage to accost them unless they themselves were the stronger party. All things were thus well arranged, and the savage whom we had in custody was awaiting the arrival of his son, who was to take his place, with the other [two] hostages.

On the third day they kept their promise and brought with them the three boys, aged from twelve to eighteen, telling us they had made great search and investigation to find out who had killed our men, but without success; however, they would see to it that in a short time they would give us information. They were greatly distressed, they added, over the misfortune that had happened to us; but, as for themselves, they were all innocent, and as such did not feel themselves to blame. They brought the three youths, the son of our prisoner, one from Tadoussac, and the third, the son of Mahigan Aticq, who all lived near our settlement, and they exonerated the Three Rivers men, saying that it could not have been any of them who had committed the murder, since there were only two wigwams of them, and on the night of the murder they were all at home. They begged us withal to live at peace with them until we should have discovered the murderers, whom it was perfectly reasonable that we should put to death; and they asked us to take good care of the savages they were leaving with us. The father whom we were holding as a prisoner said to his son: "Take care to live at peace with the French; and be quite sure that in a short time I shall deliver you, and learn who did that deed; the greatest grief I have is that the French should have suspected me." The other savages encouraged the two other youths also, telling them that in a few days the author of this wicked deed would be discovered. . . .

Towards the end of January [1628] some thirty savages, men, women, and children, pressed by hunger, owing to there being too little snow to enable them to hunt moose and other animals, resolved to come to our neighbourhood in order that in their extreme necessity they might get relief in the way of provisions, without which they must perish. I again pointed out what a detestable act the murder of our men was, and how richly the murderer deserved punishment for his deed; that on his account they might all suffer and die of hunger, if they were cut off from the assistance of our settlement and the kindness of the French, from whom they received only benefits of every kind. The starving band, desirous of testifying the resentment they felt respecting the death of our men, and their complete innocence of any participation in that act of perfidy, desiring also to join with us in a closer friendship than ever before, and to remove any distrust of them we could possibly have, decided to give us three girls of the ages of eleven, twelve, and fifteen, to dispose of as we might consider best, and have them educated and treated like those of our own nation, and have them marry if it seemed good to us to do so. . . .

After having heard all they had to say, I judged that, for the greater security of those who were dwelling in this country, and to establish a closer friendship, it would not be inexpedient to accept this offer, and to take the girls. This was something they had never offered before, no matter what present we should have been willing to give them to have one of their girls. Indeed, even the surgeon, some time before, desiring to have a young girl in order to have her educated and afterwards to marry her, could not persuade any of the savages to let him have one, no matter what he offered; although his whole object was the glory of God, in his great desire to rescue one of the souls of this land from hell. In truth I was greatly surprised at their offer, which, as I have said above, was such as we had never before been able to obtain from them.

16

SAMUEL DE CHAMPLAIN

An English Blockade Threatens
Québec's Survival

1628

*The arrival of the English in the Saint Lawrence Valley soon presented
Champlain with an even more dangerous crisis than the tensions with
the Natives during the autumn of 1627 (discussed in Document 15). In
1627 the Kirke family obtained a commission from Charles I of England
authorizing them to seize control of New France in his name. Jarvis
Kirke then sent a fleet under the command of David Kirke to establish a
blockade of the Saint Lawrence River and waylay the fleet bringing supplies in the spring of 1628 to the French colony at Québec. By this means
they intended to starve the French colony into submission. They also took
control of the fur trade in the Saint Lawrence Valley. The Kirkes received
significant assistance from Basque fishermen and fur traders and from
renegade French traders in the region who were angry that the French
crown had abolished free trade in New France and established royal
monopoly companies controlling the fur trade.*

*Even before the English ships actually arrived, Champlain faced a
dire situation, as supplies were running low and he knew that he could
not hold out indefinitely if supply ships from France did not arrive soon.
Despite Champlain's efforts to prod the shareholders in France to sponsor settlers and encourage cultivation in New France, the colony was
nowhere near self-sufficient in food. Loath to accede to Thomas Kirke's
demand that he capitulate, Champlain decided to attempt a bluff and
hold out for another year in hopes that the situation would change in
Europe and the English would be forced to withdraw. As he describes
in this section of his* The Second Part of the Voyages of the Sieur de
Champlain *(1632), Champlain then attempted to prepare the colony for
an even more difficult winter ahead.*

Samuel de Champlain, *The Second Part of the Voyages of the Sieur de Champlain* (1632),
vol. 5, bk. 2, trans. W. D. Lesueur, in *The Works of Samuel de Champlain*, ed. Henry
Percival Biggar et al. (Toronto: Champlain Society, 1922–1935; Toronto: University of
Toronto Press, 1971), 265–87.

On the eighteenth of the same month [June] La Fourière [a Montagnais chief from Tadoussac] returned to barter for provisions and tobacco: on this trip he did not give himself as much trouble about the prisoner as he had done on the former occasion. He told us that he had yet not heard of any vessels having arrived off the coast, which made us anxious since all our provisions were exhausted, excepting four or five barrels of quite poor biscuit, which was not much, and some peas and beans, to which we were now reduced, without any other commodities. Such are the straits to which we are brought every year, to say nothing of the possible unhappy consequences. I have already fully pointed this out in many places, and spoken of the misfortunes that have been caused by the insufficiency of our supplies. Now we were waiting for news from day to day, not knowing what to think, considering the condition of want in which we might be—in which we were, in fact—and that the vessels ought to have arrived with relief for us by the end of May at the latest. We could only conjecture that some change might have been made in connection with the business of the Company; or that the vessels had met with contrary winds. . . .

On the ninth of July two of our men came on foot from Cape Tourmente, bringing news of the arrival of six vessels at Tadoussac, according to the report of an Indian, who himself the same day confirmed the statement, adding that a man from Dieppe, named Captain Michel, was in command on behalf of the Sieur de Caen. This information made us think that it might be the man who was part owner of the vessel with de Caen, and who usually came to Gaspé to fish for cod. This news cheered us up somewhat. On the other hand, considering that there were six vessels, an extraordinary circumstance in one of these trading voyages, it did not seem probable that this Captain Michel was in command of the fleet, since he was not the kind of person for so important a command; and so we were brought to the conclusion that there was some more or less extraordinary change in what was going on. The savage, besides, on being particularly questioned, told us a number of stories that were inconsistent: among others, that these ships had captured a Basque vessel which was trading at Isle Percée, and that they traded its goods with the savages at Tadoussac. Desiring to know the truth more fully, we decided to ask a young interpreter, a Greek by race, if he could disguise himself as an Indian, and go in a canoe to discover what vessels these could be. We offered him two savages to go with him, in whose fidelity we had confidence, and who promised to serve us in this affair if we would present them with some gratuity. The Greek resolved to embark on the expedition, and when we had provided him with everything necessary, he set out.

Meanwhile I was distrustful, fearing what I had often apprehended, and what I had often given warning of, namely: that these were enemies; which caused me to put both the settlement and the fort in order, so that we might be prepared to receive the enemy, if such he was.

And now, only an hour after the Greek had gone, he returns with two canoes which were seeking refuge at our settlement, in one of which was Foucher, who was staying at Cape Tourmente to look after the men that were settled there. He told us that he had escaped from the hands of the English, who had made him prisoner with three of his men, a woman, and a little girl, whom they had taken on board a boat anchored off the said Cape Tourmente, after having killed what cattle they wanted and burnt the rest in their stables, where they had shut them up. They had also burnt two small houses into which Foucher and his men had retired, and had destroyed everything they could, even to the caps worn by the little girl. . . .

Being now only too sure that the enemy [the English] was at hand, I set all hands to work to make entrenchments around the settlement, and barricades on the ramparts of the fort which were not completed, no work having been done on them since the departure of the vessels, on account of the small number of our labourers, whose time had been quite taken up during the winter in providing firewood. These things having been accomplished in all haste, I assigned the men to the places which I judged suitable, so that each might know his own post, and hasten to it according to the necessity of the moment.

The next day, the tenth of the month [July 1628], about three in the afternoon, we saw a boat which seemed, from the manoeuvres it was making, to want to go into the river St. Charles, with the object of making a descent, or setting fire to the houses of the Fathers; or else they did not know the right course to take to come straight to our settlement. This boat, I judged, could not accomplish much unless others came as well, and it seemed unlikely that it had come in this reckless fashion, because those on board might expect that most of them would never get away alive. Some other object must therefore have brought them. At the same time I did not want to neglect any measure of precaution, and I sent some men armed with arquebuses into the woods to watch where they were going to land, and wait resolutely for them there in order to resist their landing and defeat them if possible. As they were approaching the land, our men recognized some of our own people on board, with a woman and her little girl, which reassured them. Some of our men, coming into the open, told them to land at the settlement; which they did, when we recognized that they were Basques. They were prisoners of the English, who had sent this boat to carry back our people, and deliver a letter from the General. One of the Basques whom I bade to come ashore, and who had the letter, said to me: "Sir, the compulsory command which we have from the English General, who is lying off Tadoussac, has obliged us to come here and deliver this letter to you from him, which you will be good enough to read, if you please. I beg of you to pardon and excuse us; for we are acting under compulsion." I took the letter, and brought in the Basques, six in number, to whom I offered good entertainment [food and drink] while they were waiting to be sent away. It was now quite late, and consequently they did not go back till the next morning.

The letter was read in the presence of the Sieur du Pont and myself and some others of our principal residents, whom I had summoned to take counsel as to what reply we should make. The letter was as follows: —

Sirs, I give you notice that I have obtained a Commission from the King of Great Britain, my most honoured Lord and Master, to take possession of these countries, to wit: Canada and Acadia; and for that purpose we have set out eighteen sail strong, each vessel of which has taken its course as ordered by his Majesty. For my part, I have already seized the establishment at Miscou, and all the small craft and boats along that coast, as also those here at Tadoussac, where I am at present at anchor. You will also take notice that among the vessels that I have taken is one belonging to the New Company, which was on its way to you with provisions and refreshments, as well as goods for trading purposes, and which was under the command of a man named Norot: the Sieur de La Tour was also on board and was coming to you; which ship I have boarded from my own vessel. I had made preparations for going to see you myself, but I have thought it better only to send an advice-boat and two shallops to destroy and seize the cattle at Cape Tourmente; for I know that when you are distressed for want of food, I shall more easily obtain what I desire — which is, to take your settlement. And in order to prevent any ship arriving, I am determined to remain here until the season of navigation has closed, so that no ship may come to revictual you. Wherefore now consider what you wish to do: whether you are willing to surrender the settlement or not; for, sooner or later, with God's help, I must have it, and I should desire for your sake that it might be rather with a good grace than on compulsion, so as to avoid the bloodshed that might occur upon both sides. If you surrender the place with courtesy, you may rest assured of receiving good treatment in every respect, both as regards your persons and your goods, which latter, on my faith and on my hope of paradise, I shall preserve as carefully as if they were my own, without diminishing them by the smallest possible portion. These Basques that I send you are men from the ships I have taken; and they will be able to tell you how the affairs of France and England are going on, and even the course affairs are taking in France touching the New Company created for this country. Send me word what you wish to do; and if you desire to treat with me in this matter, send me a man for that purpose, whom I promise to treat as well as myself, giving him every kind of satisfaction, and to grant any reasonable requests you may make, on your resolving to give over to me the settlement. Awaiting your reply, and your decision to do as above expressed, I shall remain, Sirs, (and on a lower line) your affectionate servant, DAVID KIRKE, On board the Vicaille, this eighteenth of July, 1628, old style, and new style this eighth of July. (And at the head of the missive was written) To Monsieur, Monsieur de Champlain, commanding at Quebec.

The reading having been finished, the conclusion we came to about his message was that, if he wanted to see us closer at hand, he ought to come here, and not menace us from such a distance, which caused us to decide to make him the following reply: —

Sir, We entertain no doubt as to the commissions which you have obtained from the King of Great Britain. Great Princes always choose men of brave and generous disposition, amongst the number of whom he has selected you to fulfil the duty he has assigned to you for the purpose of carrying out his commands; while, on your side, you do us the favour of particularizing them, amongst others the capture of Norot and of La Tour, who was bringing out our supplies. It is true that the better a fortified place is provisioned, the better it holds out against the storms of time; nevertheless the place can make good its defence upon slender supplies when good order is maintained in it. That is the reason why, having still grain, Indian corn, peas, and beans, not to mention what this country produces, a diet that the soldiers of this place can content themselves with as well as they could with the finest kinds of flour in the world; and knowing well that, were we to surrender a fort and a settlement conditioned as we now are, we should not be worthy of the name of men in the presence of our King, but rather be reprehensible and merit chastisement in the sight of God and men, honour demands that we fight to the death. For these reasons I know that you will think more highly of our courage if we firmly await the arrival of yourself and your forces than if, in a cowardly fashion, we abandoned something that is so dear to us without first making proof of your cannon, your approaches, entrenchments, and battery against a place which I am confident, when you see and reconnoitre it, you will not judge to be so easy of access as perhaps you have been led to believe, nor its defenders to be persons destitute of courage to defend it, seeing they are men who have tried the hazards of fortune in many different places. Then if the issue is favourable to you, you will have more cause, having vanquished us, to bestow your offers of kind treatment, than if [without a struggle] we placed you in possession of a place the preservation of which is enjoined upon us by the strongest considerations of duty that can be imagined. So far as the destruction at Cape Tourmente and the burning of our cattle is concerned, this was only a little thatched building with four or five men in charge, who were taken unawares by the help of the savages. It is a matter of a few beasts dead which in no way diminish what we depend upon for our living; and had you come a day later, there would have been nothing for you to do [at that place]. We are now waiting from hour to hour to receive you, and resist, if we can, the claims you are making to these places, exempt from which I shall remain, Sir, (and lower down) Your affectionate servant, CHAMPLAIN (and above) To Monsieur, Monsieur the General KIRKE, of the English vessels.

When this reply was finished, I gave it to the Basques, who went back; and I sent a boat to Cape Tourmente to see the ruin the English had left behind them, and find out whether any of the cattle had escaped. Some six cows had been left, but these the savages had killed; and one, which had escaped by running away into the woods, was brought back.

The Basques on arriving at Tadoussac gave my letter to General Kirke, whom we were awaiting from day to day. After having made enquiries of the Basques, he assembled all the men of his vessels, and particularly those in command, to whom he read the letter. Thereupon they decided not to waste time, as they saw that there was nothing to be done; for they believed that we were better supplied with provisions and munitions of war than we really were, each man of us at the time being reduced to seven ounces of peas a day, while of gunpowder we had only 50 lbs., with very little in the way of fuse or any other supplies; so that, if they had pushed on, it would have been very hard for us to resist them, because of the wretched condition we were in; which shows that on such occasions it is a good thing to put on a bold countenance. During this time we kept careful watch, my companions being continually on duty. Kirke not caring to wait any longer for our vessels, which he believed had all been either lost or captured, decided to burn all our pinnaces at Tadoussac; and this they did, with the exception of the largest, which they carried off. Then they weighed anchor and got under way to go and look for vessels along the coast, in order to pay for the cost of their expedition.

A Chronology of the Life of
Samuel de Champlain
(1570–1635)

ca.
1570   Samuel Champlain is born in Brouage, France, to Huguenot (French Protestant) parents, Anthoine Champlain, a navy captain, and Marguerite Le Roy.

1595–
1598   Champlain is employed in the Breton branch of the royal army, as a quartermaster and eventually sergeant-in-arms. He probably converted to Catholicism around this time.

1598   *April 13*   Edict of Nantes signed, ending the French Wars of Religion.

July   Champlain accompanies his uncle, Guillaume Allène, known as the "Capitaine Provençal," to Spain, aboard Allène's ship, the *Saint-Julien*.

1599–
1601   Champlain sails with the *Saint-Julien* to the West Indies, where he travels around the Caribbean and the Gulf of Mexico. He records his observations in the *Brief Narrative*, which he presents to King Henri IV.

1603   *March 15*   Champlain sails to New France as an observer on the *Bonne Renommée*.

May–June   Champlain observes the fur trade at Tadoussac and witnesses a *tabagie* (feast) at which the French and the Montagnais and their Indian allies seal a historic pact. Champlain explores the Saint Lawrence River as far as the Lachine Rapids.

September 20   Champlain is back in Paris, where he presents Henri IV with a map of the Saint Lawrence region and publishes *Of Savages, or Voyage of Samuel Champlain of Brouage, Made to New France in the Year 1603*.

November 8   Aymar de Chaste having died, Pierre Dugua, Sieur de Mons, is made lieutenant general of Acadia and receives a royal commission to establish a settlement there.

1604   *April 7*   Champlain again sails for New France, under the command of de Mons.

May–September   De Mons and Champlain explore the coasts of Acadia, including the Bay of Fundy, and of Norumbega (the coasts of New Brunswick and Maine), including the Penobscot River.

1604– 1605   The French endure a very hard winter on Saint Croix Island — around thirty-six out of the seventy-nine men die, mostly of scurvy.

1605   *June–September*   Upon the return of Pont-Gravé from France with fresh supplies, the survivors explore the coastline as far as present-day Cape Cod, Massachusetts. They decide to winter at Port-Royal in Annapolis Bay (Nova Scotia).

1606   *June*   Poutrincourt arrives with settlers and supplies, and replaces Pont-Gravé as commander at Port-Royal.

Champlain and Poutrincourt explore the coast from Acadia to Cape Cod.

1606– 1607   Champlain and Poutrincourt return to Acadia and spend the winter at Port-Royal, where a milder winter than usual and the Order of Good Cheer improve morale and reduce casualties from scurvy.

1607   *September*   Henri VI rescinds de Mons's monopoly.

Champlain publishes a map of the Atlantic coast from Acadia to Nantucket Sound.

1608   *January*   De Mons receives a one-year extension of his monopoly and forms a trading company, in which Champlain becomes a shareholder.

January 7   De Mons and Champlain embark on what is Champlain's third crossing to New France.

July   Champlain founds Québec.

1609   *June–July*   Champlain explores the Richelieu River as far as Lake Champlain, the first European to do so, with his Indian allies and participates in a battle with the Iroquois at Ticonderoga.

October   Champlain returns to France and presents his report to de Mons and Henri IV at Fontainebleau.

1610   *April*   Champlain makes his fourth crossing to New France.

June 14–19   Champlain returns to Lake Champlain. He engages in his second battle against the Iroquois with his Indian allies.

December   Champlain enters a marriage contract with Hélène Boullé.

1611   *March*   Champlain departs for New France for the fifth time.

September   Champlain returns to France, and upon learning that de Mons and his partners have not succeeded in obtaining a new trading monopoly, he publishes a map and with de Mons's encouragement seeks a more powerful patron for New France.

1612   *November*   Upon the death of the Count of Soissons, the Prince of Condé becomes viceroy of New France and confirms Champlain's position as lieutenant for the viceroy at Québec.

1613   *March*   Champlain embarks on his sixth crossing to New France.

May–June   Champlain explores the Ottawa River region from Sault Saint-Louis to Allumette Lake in the company of interpreter Nicolas de Vignau. The Ottawa welcome him but prevent him from continuing as far as Lake Nipissing and Huronia.

Autumn   Champlain returns to France and becomes a share-holder in a new trading company, the "Canada Company," comprised of merchants from Rouen and Saint-Malo.

December (to March 1614)   Publication of *The Voyages of the Sieur de Champlain of Saintonge, Captain in the Ordinary for the King in the Navy* and the *Fourth Voyage of the Sieur de Champlain, Captain in Ordinary for the King in the Navy*, and a map, *Geographical Map of New France*.

1615   *Spring*   Champlain makes his seventh crossing to New France in the company of four Récollet missionaries.

Summer   Champlain, accompanied by two Frenchmen and Indian guides, reaches Huron country (Georgian Bay, Lake Huron) via the Ottawa River and Lake Nipissing.

Autumn   Champlain departs with Huron and Algonquin warriors to attack the Iroquois south of Lake Ontario, near Lake Oneida. Champlain is wounded and they fail to take the Iroquois fort.

1615–1616   Champlain spends the winter with the Huron based in Cahiagué (near Lake Simcoe, Ontario).

1616   *Autumn*   Champlain returns to New France and discovers that a new viceroy, the Marquis de Thémines, has replaced the dis-graced Condé. Thémines confirms Champlain as lieutenant of the viceroy.

1617   *Summer*   In June Champlain arrives in New France for a very brief visit after his eighth crossing.

1618   *February–March*   Champlain authors petitions to the Paris Chamber of Commerce and the king outlining his plans for the colony in New France and requesting assistance. The chamber and the king are supportive and accord a new monopoly to Champlain and his partners to defray the costs of sending more colonists.

Summer   After his ninth crossing to New France, Champlain spends most of the summer in administrative duties, including dealing with the murder of a French locksmith committed by two Montagnais.

Autumn   Champlain returns to France.

1619   Although the king gives Champlain a pension of 600 *livres* (French pounds) and confirms his mandate as lieutenant of the viceroy, the merchants prevent Champlain and his wife from embarking for New France. They seek to scuttle the provision that their company support colonists in New France.

May   Champlain returns to Paris and publishes *Voyages and Discoveries Made in New France, from the Year 1615 until the End of the Year 1618.*

1620   Both the new viceroy and Louis XIII confirm yet again Champlain's mandate to govern New France in their names.

Champlain makes his tenth trip to New France; he is accompanied by his wife.

1621   *Spring–Summer*   Champlain works during the spring and summer of 1621 to broker peace between the Natives and the settlers and between Pont-Gravé, representative of the old company, and Guillaume de Caën.

1621–   Champlain devotes much of his time to attempting to arrange a
1624   peace treaty between the Iroquois and the Indian allies of the French and to improving the fortifications and infrastructure of the colony.

1624   *August*   Champlain and Hélène depart for France.

1625   A new viceroy, Henri de Lévis, duke of Ventadour, replaces Montmorency. He confirms Champlain as his lieutenant.

First Jesuit monastery is founded in New France.

1626   Champlain makes his eleventh crossing to New France.

October   Cardinal Richelieu, Louis XIII's chief minister, appoints himself "grand master, chief, and general superintendent of navigation and trade" and assumes control of New France.

1627   *April*   Richelieu forms a new company, the Company of New France (or Company of the One Hundred Associates), and Champlain becomes a partner.

1628 *Spring* The Kirke brothers capture the convoy sent from Dieppe to resupply the French in New France. Champlain refuses to surrender even though supplies are low.

1629 *March 21* Cardinal Richelieu appoints Champlain "commander in New France" in Richelieu's name.

April 24 The Treaty of Susa is signed, officially ending the French-English conflict.

July 19 The English blockade prevents French supply ships from reaching Québec, and Champlain is forced to surrender the settlement.

October 29 Champlain arrives in England and files a formal complaint with the French ambassador in London.

1632 Champlain lobbies the court to act on the illegal seizure of Québec.

March With the signing of the Treaty of Saint-Germain-en-Laye the colony is finally officially returned to France, and during the summer of 1632 the English evacuate New France.

Champlain publishes his fourth and fifth works, bound in a single volume: *Voyages to Western New France, Called Canada* and *Treatise on Seamanship and the Duty of a Good Seaman.*

1633 Champlain makes his twelfth and final crossing to New France and immediately sets about repairing the fort and settlement at Québec. He resumes friendly relations with the Hurons, although tensions are higher between the French and the Algonquins and Montagnais who traded with the English during the occupation.

1635 Champlain dies on Christmas Day, 1635.

Questions for Consideration

1. How does Champlain construct his narrative voice in his writing? What role does the narrator play? How does this construction advance the goals he sought to achieve in publishing his works? To what extent is the neutral narrator of Champlain's works really an illusion? What is the purpose of that illusion? (Documents 2, 7, 8, 14, and 15)

2. How did Champlain's goals and ambitions for New France shape how he perceived and described the New World, in terms of its geography, flora, and fauna? How does his perspective differ from what we might expect of an explorer or geographer from our own culture? (Document 1)

3. What does the episode described in Document 2 demonstrate about the difficulties inherent in reconstructing history even using eyewitness accounts? What motives did each party have for concealing some or all of the truth regarding whether or not Vignau had visited the inland sea in the company of the Ottawa? Why was it so important to Champlain to reach that sea? Why were the Natives so determined to block his passage there?

4. Why were the Natives always the central figures in Champlain's writing about the New World, and why did he write so much about them? How accurate an observer of Native culture and society was Champlain? In what ways can he be called an early ethnographer? (Documents 1, 3, 8, and 9)

5. What were Champlain's goals in creating his maps? How are these goals reflected in the content and style of his maps? (Documents 4, 5, and 6)

6. Why was the pact of 1603 so significant for the future of New France? How and why did the 1603 pact come about? To what extent do you think it was as much a result of good luck or good timing on the part of the French as Champlain seems to think? Does Champlain comprehend the importance of the pact? Why or why not? (Document 8)

7. Why did Champlain accompany his Native allies into several battles with the Iroquois? What did he hope to gain from participating in these conflicts? What were the potential risks? (Documents 11 and 12)

8. Why was it so difficult for Champlain to establish a successful agricultural colony in New France? What obstacles did he encounter, and what strategies did he use to overcome them? To what extent were these obstacles structural, embedded in the very nature of the French colonial enterprise? (Documents 13, 14, and 16)

9. Why is there "no comparison" between Champlain's maps and those of his contemporaries and predecessors? What made his maps so different and groundbreaking? To what extent did his unique approach for his time derive from his education and background? How do you think this may have shaped the future of cartography and cartographical training? (Documents 3, 4, 5, and 6)

10. In what ways did Champlain seem to model his administrative style on his conceptualization of what it meant to be a good ship's captain? What qualities does he seem to have prized in a leader, and to what extent did he embody them in his own leadership of New France? (Documents 7, 13, 14, 15, and 16)

11. Why were the Kirke brothers determined to take over Québec? What did they want with New France? To what extent did they share Champlain's vision? What, if anything, could Champlain have done to avoid the debacle in 1628–1629? What does his handling of the situation tell us about his skills as an administrator and a diplomat? (Document 16)

12. Why was Champlain so consistently interested in the alliances and enmities among the Native peoples? Why did he think it vital, for example, to reconcile the Montagnais and the Huron with the Iroquois? What do you think was the likelihood that he would be able to broker a lasting peace among these peoples? (Documents 1, 10, and 11)

13. What was the cause of the conflict between Champlain and his Montagnais allies in Document 15? Why was the conflict so difficult to resolve? In the end, who seems to have gotten the upper hand in the standoff? Why?

14. How did Champlain understand Native religions? To what extent did his conceptualization of them reflect the reality of Native beliefs? To what extent is it likely that Champlain and Anadabijou understood each other's explanation of their respective religious beliefs? (Documents 8, 9, 10, 11, and 12)

15. How did Champlain's ideas regarding military tactics and strategies differ from those of the Natives? To what extent were those differences rooted in divergent ideas about the purpose of warfare itself? Explain. (Documents 11 and 12)

Selected Bibliography

Biggar, Henry Percival, et al., general ed., W. F. Ganong, J. Home Cameron, H. H. Langton, W. D. Lesueur, J. Squair, eds. *The Works of Samuel de Champlain.* 6 vols. Toronto: Champlain Society, 1922–1935. Reprint, University of Toronto Press, 1971.

Thwaites, Reuben Gold, ed. *The Jesuit Relations and Allied Documents: Travels and Explorations of the Jesuit Missionaries in New France 1610–1791.* 73 vols. Cleveland, 1896–1901. Reprint, New York: Pageant Book Company, 1959.

BIOGRAPHIES OF CHAMPLAIN

Armstrong, Joe C. W. *Champlain.* Toronto: Macmillan of Canada, 1987.

Armstrong, Joe C. W. *Samuel de Champlain.* Translated by Normand Paiement and Christiane Lacroix. Montreal: Les Éditions de l'Homme, 1988.

Bishop, Morris. *Champlain: The Life of Fortitude.* London: Macdonald, 1949.

Hackett Fischer, David. *Champlain's Dream.* New York: Simon & Schuster, 2008. (This work contains a comprehensive bibliography of primary and secondary sources related to Champlain.)

Morison, Samuel Eliot. *Samuel de Champlain: Father of New France.* New York: Little, Brown, 1972.

Séguin, Maurice K. *Samuel de Champlain: L'entrepreneur et le rêveur.* Sillery, Québec: Les Éditions du Septentrion, 2008.

OTHER SECONDARY SOURCES (ENGLISH)

Biggar, Henry Percival. *The Early Trading Companies of New France: A Contribution to the History of Commerce and Discovery in North America.* Toronto: University of Toronto Press, 1901.

Brazeau, Brian. *Writing a New France, 1604–1632 (Transculturalisms, 1400–1700).* Aldershot, U.K.: Ashgate, 2009.

Brunelle, Gayle K. *The New World Merchants of Rouen, 1559–1630.* Sixteenth Century Essays and Studies, vol. 16. Kirksville, Mo.: Sixteenth Century Journal Publishers, 1991.

Delâge, Denys. *Bitter Feast: Amerindians and Europeans in Northeastern North America, 1600–1664.* Translated by Jane Brierley. Vancouver: University of British Columbia Press, 1993.

Heidenreich, Conrad E. *Explorations and Mapping of Samuel de Champlain 1603–1632.* Monograph no. 17. *Cartographica* (1976).

Holt, Mack P. *The French Wars of Religion, 1562–1669.* 2nd ed. New Approaches to European History. Cambridge, U.K.: Cambridge University Press, 2005.

Hunter, Douglas. *God's Mercies: Rivalry, Betrayal, and the Dream of Discovery.* Toronto: Doubleday Canada, 2007.

Innis, Harold A. *The Fur Trade in Canada: An Introduction to Canadian Economic History.* Revised edition. New Haven, Conn.: Yale University Press, 1962.

Jaenen, Cornelius J. *Friend and Foe: Aspects of French-Amerindian Cultural Contact in the Sixteenth and Seventeenth Centuries.* New York: Columbia University Press, 1976.

Litalien, Raymonde, and Denis Vaugeois, eds. *Champlain: The Birth of French America.* Translated by Käthe Roth. Montréal: McGill-Queen's University Press, 2004.

Litalien, Raymonde, Jean-François Palomino, and Denis Vaugeois. *Mapping a Continent: Historical Atlas of North America 1492–1814.* Translated by Käthe Roth. Québec: Septentrion/McGill-Queen's University Press, 2007.

Moussette, Marcel. "A Universe Under Strain: Amerindian Nations in Northeastern North America in the 16th Century." *Post-Medieval Archaeology* 43, no. 1 (2009): 30–47.

Peace, Thomas G. M. "Deconstructing the Sauvage/Savage in the Writing of Samuel de Champlain and Captain John Smith." *French Colonial History* 7 (2006): 1–20.

Trigger, Bruce G. "Champlain Judged by His Indian Policy: A Different View of Early Canadian History." *Anthropologica* 13 (1971): 85–114.

———. *The Children of Aataentsic: A History of the Huron People to 1660.* Montréal: McGill-Queens University Press, 1976.

———. "The French Presence in Huronia: The Structure of Franco-Huron Relations in the First Half of the Seventeenth Century." *Canadian Historical Review* 49, no. 2 (June 1968): 107–41.

———. *Natives and Newcomers: Canada's "Heroic Age" Reconsidered.* Kingston, ON: McGill-Queen's University Press, 1985.

Trudel, Marcel. *The Beginnings of New France, 1524–1663.* Toronto: McClelland & Stewart, 1973.

SECONDARY SOURCES (FRENCH)

Allaire, Bernard. *Pelleteries, manchons et chapeaux de castor: les fourrures nord-américaines à Paris, 1500–1632.* Sillery, Québec: Les Éditions du Septentrion; Paris: Presses de l'Université de Paris-Sorbonne, 1999.

Binot, Guy. *Pierre Dugua de Mons, gentilhomme royannais, premier colonisateur du Canada, lieutenant général de la Nouvelle-France de 1603 à 1612.* Royan: Éditions Bonne Anse, 2004.

Blondel-Loisel, Annie, and Raymonde Litalien, with Jean-Paul Barbiche and Claude Briot. *De la Seine au Saint-Laurent avec Champlain.* Paris: L'Harmattan, 2005.

Bonnichon, Philippe. *Des cannibales aux castors: les découvertes françaises de l'Amérique (1503–1788).* Paris: Éditions France-Empire, 1994.

D'Avignon, Matthieu. *Champlain et les fondateurs oubliés : Les figures du père et le mythe de la fondation.* Québec: Les Presses de l'Université Laval, 2008.

Haudré, Philippe. *L'Empire des rois 1500–1789.* Paris: Éditions Denoël, 1997.

Havard, Gilles, and Cécile Vidal. *Histoire de l'Amérique française.* Paris: Éditions Flammarion, 2003.

Lemire, Maurice. "Champlain: entre l'objectivité et la subjectivité," in *Scritti sulla Nouvelle-France nel seicento. Quaderni del seicento francese*, no. 6. Bari: Adriatica, 1984. Reprint, Paris: Nizet, 1984.

Martinière, Guy, and Didier Poton, eds. *Le Nouveau Monde et Champlain.* Paris: Les Indes Savantes, 2008.

Morissonneau, Christian, Maryse Chevrette, and Isabelle Lafortune. *Le rêve américain de Champlain.* Montréal: Hurtubise, 2009.

Thierry, Éric, ed. *À la rencontre des Algonquins et des Hurons, 1612–1619.* Québec: Septentrion, 2009.

———. *Marc Lescarbot (vers 1570–1641): Un homme de plume au service de la Nouvelle-France.* Paris: Honoré Champion Éditeur, 2001.

Acknowledgments (*continued from p. iv*)

Documents 1, 2, 7–10, and 13–16: Used with permission of the Champlain Society.

Document 3: Courtesy of the Bibliothèque nationale de France.

Document 4: Courtesy of the Library of Congress.

Document 5: Courtesy of the John Carter Brown Library at Brown University.

Documents 6, 11, and 12: Text: Used with permission of the Champlain Society; images: Courtesy of the John Carter Brown Library at Brown University.

Index

Acadia
    Champlain's exploration of, 14–16, 33–37, 124
    English raid on, 19
    fur and fishing trades in, 4
    search for mines in, 13–14
    winter settlement in, 15–16, 100–104
agricultural colony
    Champlain's vision of, 2, 4, 76
    founding of Québec, 17
    fur traders' opposition to, 4–5, 14, 20, 22
Algonquins
    agriculture and, 76
    Champlain's attempt to reach Hudson Bay and, 41–48
    Champlain's military alliance with, 17–18, 41, 44, 80–88
    description of cemeteries, 43
    description of rituals, 71–72
    relations with French, 15
    wars with Iroquois, 8, 13, 67, 69, 80–88
Almouchiquois, 53
Anadabijou
    hosting of *tabagie*, 13, 68–69
    importance of, 23
    on Native beliefs, 72–74
Argall, Samuel, 19
Arte de navegar (Medina), 60
Atlantic coast
    Champlain's exploration of, 15, 33–37, 124
    Champlain's map of, 51–52, 124
Atlantic Ocean, map of, 49–50

Basque
    English blockade and, 116, 119, 121
    in fur and fishing trades, 4, 6, 14
Bessabez, 35, 36, 37
Boullé, Eustache, 16, 20, 21
Boullé, Hélène, 16, 20
Bourbon, Henri de, 7
Brief Narrative of the Most Remarkable Things that Samuel de Champlain of Brouage Observed in the West Indies, 1599–1601, 12, 123

Cabahis, 36, 37
Caën, Émery de, 20, 105
Caën, Ezéchiel de, 105

Caën, Guillaume de, 20, 105, 106, 107, 108, 109
Canada Company, 19, 125
Cape Cod, 15, 33
Cartier, Jacques, 6–7, 8, 23
Catholic League, 7
Catholics/Catholicism
    Champlain's conversion to, 10, 123
    evangelization of Natives, 2, 5, 17, 21, 76
    first church and seminary in New France, 20–21
    Jesuit missionaries, 5, 21, 126
    Récollet missionaries, 5, 17, 20–21
    Wars of Religion, 7
Champlain, Anthoine de, 10, 123
Champlain, Samuel de
    alliances with Natives, 1, 5, 13, 17–18, 23–24, 41, 44, 67–70, 80, 89
    appointment as lieutenant, 16, 18, 20, 21, 22, 125
    attempt to reach Hudson Bay, 38–48
    birth and early life of, 10, 123
    as cartographer, 2–4, 10, 11, 49, 51, 53, 60
    clashes with fur trade merchants, 14, 22
    as colonial administrator, 19–23, 100–121, 126
    crucial alliance with Montagnais, 5, 13, 67–68
    death of, 23, 127
    debate over legacy of, 1, 10
    description of Hurons, 89–99
    description of Montagnais, 68–70, 77–79, 81–88
    early expeditions to New France, 4, 12–13, 14–16, 123, 124
    English seizure of Québec and, 21–22, 116–21, 127
    explanation of mapmaking, 55–59
    exploration of Acadia, 14–16, 124
    exploration of Atlantic coast, 15, 33–37, 51–52, 124
    explorations of interior lands, 18, 19, 23, 38–48, 80–88, 124, 125
    final return to Québec, 23, 127
    focus on Saint Lawrence area, 16
    as founder of New France, 1, 23–25
    founding of Québec, 1, 17, 76–79, 124
    greatest contributions of, 1–2

135